ODDBALL MINNESOTA

A Guide to Some Really

STRANGE PLACES

JEROME POHLEN

CHICAGO
REVIEW
PRESS

03 – 1182

Library of Congress Cataloging-in-Publication Data

Pohlen, Jerome.
   Oddball Minnesota : a guide to some really strange places /
   Jerome Pohlen.—1st ed.
      p. cm.
   Includes bibliographical references (p. 223) and indexes.
   ISBN 1-55652-478-1
   1. Minnesota—Guidebooks. 2. Minnesota—History, Local—Miscellanea.
   3. Curiosities and wonders—Minnesota. I. Title
F604.3 .P64 2003
     917.7604'54—dc21

                2002015974

Cover photo: Big Ole stands guard outside the Kensington Runestone Museum in Alexandria; photo by Jerome Pohlen.

The author has made every effort to secure permissions for all the material in this book. If any acknowledgment has inadvertently been omitted, please contact the author.

All photographs courtesy of Jerome Pohlen unless otherwise noted.
Cover and interior design: Mel Kupfer

© 2003 by Jerome Pohlen
All rights reserved
First edition
Published by Chicago Review Press, Incorporated
814 North Franklin Street
Chicago, Illinois 60610
ISBN 1-55652-478-1
Printed in the United States of America
5 4 3 2 1

FOR MY GRANDPARENTS,
**JOSEPH AND
FRANCES POHLEN,**
FROM THAT GREAT STATE
TO THE SOUTH.

CONTENTS

INTRODUCTION

I've never fully understood Minnesota's state slogan: "Land of 10,000 Lakes." OK, sure, the lakes are beautiful—no, breathtaking—but what's this obsession with numbers? Don't you lose track after the first hundred or so? Why not "Land of 382 Million Trees" or "Land of 947 Billion Wildflowers"? At some point the law of diminishing returns has to kick in. It is an arithmetic fact that the more items you have in a group, the less unique each item in that group is. Arizona: "Land of 1 Lake." Now *that's* a slogan!

What if—and this is just a suggestion—Minnesota touted one of its many one-of-a-kind features? "Land of the World's Largest Prairie Chicken." "Birthplace of Spam." "Home of the World's Oldest Rock." Do you see the difference? If so, this guide is for you.

Oddball Minnesota won't waste your time telling you about attractions you can find by simply walking a mile in any direction. No lakes, no bike trails, no quaint cafés. But where did Tiny Tim strum his last notes on the ukulele? Why are two grasshoppers bowing down to the Virgin Mary in a Cold Spring chapel? Is that mummy in the McLeod County Museum from Peru . . . or outer space?!!?! *These* are the types of questions you'll have answered as you search for the strange on Minnesota's backroads.

Oh, I know it sounds crazy. But while all your friends and coworkers are spending their vacations fighting off mosquitoes in the Boundary Waters, you'll be sizing up the World's Largest Ear of Corn. While they stare for hours at holes in frozen lakes, you'll be admiring the fourth Zamboni ever built. Who's crazy now?

Well, you still are. But don't let that stop you. Put that canoe in dry dock. Hang the bike and the fishing pole in the garage. Fill up the tank and grab your atlas—the weirdness awaits!

And one last thing; there aren't 10,000 lakes in Minnesota, there are 14,215. That's 14,214 more lakes than there are six-story statues of the Jolly Green Giant. Do you need any other reason to hit the road?

While I've tried to give clear directions from major streets and landmarks, you could still make a wrong turn. Winter comes early in these parts—August, I think—so it's not a good idea to be lost for too long. Here are a few tips for getting out of a jam and making the most of your Oddball road trip:

• **Stop and ask!** For a lot of communities, their Oddball attractions might be their only claim to fame. Locals are often thrilled that you'd drive out of your way to marvel at their gigantic fiberglass creature, especially during the dead of winter. But choose your guides wisely. Old farmers at the grain elevator are a good source of information; pimply teenage clerks at Casey's General Store are not.

• **Call ahead.** Few Oddball sites keep regular hours, but most will gladly wait around if they know you're coming. Don't forget that as soon as the lakes freeze over, the folks who run these strange attractions are out snowmobiling, ice fishing, or digging out of snowdrifts. Always call.

• **Recheck your compass.** Many towns in Minnesota, for reasons that might *seem* practical but end up being infuriating, repeat their numbered street names. In a town that consists of only 25 blocks, it is not uncommon to find two First Streets and two First Avenues. East–west running First Streets are distinguished from one another by being named First Street N and First Street S, both one block from Main Street. In other words, you'll find four very similar street addresses: 101 E. First Street N, 101 W. First Street N, 101 E. First Street S, and 101 W. First Street S. Add into the equation north–south running avenues, east and west of, say, Center Street—101 N. First Avenue E, 101 S. First Avenue E, 101 N. First Avenue W, and 101 S. First Avenue W—well, you get the picture. Start banging your head on the dashboard now.

• **Don't give up.** It is no small feat to raise $12,000 for a 21-foot-long floating loon to put on the town's lake, to say nothing of maintaining it so it doesn't sink. These communities never gave up, and neither should you.

• **Don't trespass!** Don't become a Terrible Tourist. Don't climb on the statues. Don't trespass on private land. When in doubt, ask permission, or stay on the road.

Do you have an Oddball site of your own? Have I missed anything? Do you know of a location that should be included in a later edition? Please write and let me know: Chicago Review Press, 814 N. Franklin Street, Chicago, IL 60610.

THE NORThWEST

So where should you start your quest for Minnesota's odd-balls? Perhaps at Minnesota's Northwest Angle on the Lake of the Woods. Jutting up above the 49th Parallel, this geographic anomaly is the northernmost point of the continental United States. Unfortunately, it is accessible only through Canada; it might as well be in a foreign country. (Maybe that's why its few residents have threatened to secede from the union.)

Still, the northwestern part of the state has plenty of easily accessed weirdness, most of it enormous and hard to miss. This comes in handy if you're not good with maps. The region also has the state's highest concentration of Paul Bunyanalia—red-flanneled statues, oversized artifacts, jilted sweethearts, abandoned logging tools, and toenail clippings. You can even find Bunyan's grave up here.

But that's not all that's strange and out of proportion. There must be growth hormones in the water; you'll also find mammoth mallards and otters and prairie chickens and crows and grasshoppers and pelicans and coots—you start to wonder whether this stuff is truly big, or whether you've just shrunk!

Hop on up!

Akeley
Paul Bunyan Town

Bangor, Maine, claims to be the birthplace of Paul Bunyan, but it hardly has as valid a claim as Akeley, Minnesota. You see, Paul wasn't so much born as he was conceived—and not as long ago as you might think. The big guy was mostly the invention of William B. Laughead, a PR hack for the Red River Lumber Company, which had its largest sawmill in Akeley. Starting in 1914—that's right, Paul Bunyan is younger than the airplane—Laughead churned out pulp novels of the hero's exploits for American schoolchildren. Kids adored the oversized, fun-lovin' lumberjack chopping through our nation's forests. Never mind that in reality the woods were being laid to waste by a vast timber conglomerate. Laughead also invented Babe the Blue Ox, Big Ole, Johnny Inkslinger, and Paul's dog Sport.

The best place to learn about Paul Bunyan and the history of the Red River Lumber Company is at Paul's Cabin, a museum you enter through a Phillips 66 station on the east side of Akeley. Owner Nels Kramer will likely be there to show you his extensive collection of Red River memorabilia.

The museum is shaped like a starfish with exhibits radiating out from a central display area. One wing has an elaborate model of Akeley during the heyday of the Red River lumber mill, circa 1905. Another wing contains a miniature logging camp and Minnesota farm, and the next has a collection of tools and transportation, including a working model train. The best wing, however, is dedicated to Paul Bunyan—the guy in red flannel, the one created by Laughead, the one whose mustache looks almost like a cat's whiskers.

Paul's Cabin/Red River Museum, 440 E. Broadway, Akeley, MN 56433
(218) 652-2588 or (218) 652-3333
Hours: May–September, Tuesday–Saturday 10 A.M.–6 P.M., Sunday Noon–5 P.M.; other
  times by appointment
Cost: Adults $3, Kids $1
Directions: On Rte. 34 (Broadway), just west of the Rte. 64 turnoff to Bemidji.

Paul's Cabin was not the first museum to open in this town. Another is located behind the town's big Bunyan statue and is staffed by volunteers from the local historical society. The structure is dwarfed by a 28-foot fiberglass statue kneeling on the lawn out front. Crafted by Dean Krotzer in 1984, this Paul, if he were able to stand erect, would be 50 feet tall. The statue is by far Minnesota's most photo-friendly Bunyan monument—mostly because he holds out an upturned palm for you to sit on. Your coworkers will no doubt show you a little more respect when you pass around vacation pics of you and your gigantic, ax-wielding friend.

Just behind the statue is Paul's baby cradle, protected from the elements by a wooden canopy. Another colossal cradle is located on a lot across the street next to the Woodtick Musical Theatre. Still want more Bunyanalia? Drop by Akeley during the last weekend in June each year for Paul Bunyan Days.

Paul Bunyan Statue and Museum, Memorial Park, Broadway & Chicago Ave., Akeley, MN 56433

Contact: Paul Bunyan Historical Society, PO Box 131, Akeley, MN 46433

(218) 652-2575

Hours: Always visible; Museum May–September, Tuesday–Sunday 10 A.M.–5 P.M.

Cost: Free

www.akeleyminnesota.com

Directions: On Rte. 34 (Broadway), just west of the Rte. 64 turnoff to St. Cloud.

Alexandria
The Kensington Runestone

Do you think Columbus discovered the New World? Well, you'd better keep that ill-informed opinion to yourself if you plan to visit Alexandria, known in these parts as the Birthplace of America. One hundred and thirty years before that misguided Italian navigator stepped onto the beach at San Salvador and proclaimed he'd reached India, a group of Vikings had already penetrated the continent to present-day Minnesota and their eventual demise.

What proof is there of this early voyage? On November 8, 1898, farmer Olof Ohman dug up a 202-pound stone on his property north of Kensington. The flat graywacke slab was tangled in the roots of a 40-year-old aspen tree he was clearing for a new field. Ohman noticed it was covered with strange, chiseled markings so he brought it back to his farm.

Kensington Runestone Discovery Site, County Road 103, Kensington, MN 56343

No phone

Hours: Always visible

Cost: Free

Directions: North two miles from Kensington on Rte. 1, right on Rte. 103 (Runestone Lane), then north at the first left (still Rte. 103); one mile ahead.

ALEXANDRIA

Alexandria men with garlic, onions, or sardines on their breath may not, by law, have intercourse with their wives.

Columbus who?

Ohman planned to use the stone as a doorstop, but he also brought it to the attention of a local newspaper editor who sent a sketch of the markings to the University of Minnesota to be translated. The scratches turned out to be runes, and they translated roughly as:

8 Goths [Swedes] and 22 Norwegians on exploration journey from Vinland over the West. We had camp by 2 skerries [islands] one days journey north from this stone. We were and fished one day. After we came home found 10 men red with blood and dead. Ave Virgo Maria, save from evil. . . . Have 10 of our party by sea to look after our ships 14 days journey from this island. Year 1362.

The translator also suggested the rock resembled the type used as ballast in Viking ships. The stone was further studied at several universities around the Midwest.

Shortly after being proclaimed the biggest find since the Rosetta Stone, others denounced the Kensington Runestone as a clever but obvious fraud. Battle lines were drawn with Scandinavians on one side and non-Scandinavians on the other. (Some doubters claim the text was lifted from *The Well-Informed Schoolmaster* by Carl Rosland.) The debate got personal, by calling into question Ohman's veracity. Angered, the old farmer retrieved his stone, brought it home, and used it as an anvil. One of Ohman's sons eventually committed suicide after suffering years of ridicule, and Ohman's daughter fled town. (About this same time, a neighboring farmer found another runestone but, seeing the grief it brought Ohman, reburied the tablet. It has yet to be rediscovered.)

That might have been the end of the story, but the Smithsonian became interested in settling the question in the late 1940s. They must have thought the runestone genuine, for it was put on display in Washington in 1948.

Piggybacking on the publicity, the Alexandria Kiwanis Club commissioned an oversized granite replica in 1951. You can still see the 25-foot stone in Runestone Park, one mile east of town on Route 27 (east of McKay Avenue). The replica was followed by a 28-foot, 4-ton Viking statue of Ole Oppe, better known as Big Ole. Both went to the 1964 New York World's Fair. Big Ole was built by Gordon Schumaker and today stands in the middle of Broadway in Alexandria—in front of the museum at Third Street—you can't miss him.

In the late 1960s, the Smithsonian issued its revised verdict: the

Kensington Runestone was a fake. It was returned to Minnesota for the final time. When it arrived, locals became suspicious after discovering the Smithsonian had scrubbed the stone with a wire brush, thereby destroying any microevidence that could have dated it. Was it just a bonehead move, or was the nation's most revered museum involved in a Columbus-centric cover-up? Something still smells fishy, for although the Smithsonian to this day cites "experts" in its literature denouncing the stone, it has yet to identify who those experts were.

You're just going to have to make up your own mind. The Runestone Museum makes a compelling case, though it does not ignore conflicting claims. In that respect, it's more fair than the Smithsonian.

Kensington Runestone Museum, 206 N. Broadway, Alexandria, MN 56308

(320) 763-3160

E-mail: bigole@rea-alp.com

Hours: April–September, Monday–Friday 9 A.M.–5 P.M., Saturday 9 A.M.–4 P.M., Sunday 11 A.M.–4 P.M.; October–March, Monday–Friday 9 A.M.–5 P.M., Saturday 9 A.M.–3 P.M.

Cost: Adults $5, Seniors $4, Kids (7–17) $3

www.runestonemuseum.org

Resources: www.geocities.com/TheTropics/Island/3634/index2.html

www.geocities.com/Athens/Aegean/6726/kensington/kensington.htm

Directions: Exit 103 from I-94, go north on Rte. 29 (Broadway) until you see Big Ole at Second Ave.

THE NORWAY LAKE RUNESTONE?

Some Minnesotans believe another Viking runestone is located some-where beneath the surface of Norway Lake near Sunburg. Witnesses have reported a large, carved rock on an island that appears at the center of Lower Norway Lake during droughts. Farmer Elmer Roen spotted the markings in 1938 and described the stone as at least 20 square feet and covered in runic letters. Divers have not been able to find the flat stone, though they've tried several times. To learn the latest details, contact the Viking Research Society of Minnesota (Route 1, PO Box 60, Chokio, MN 56221).

Ashby
World's Largest Coot

It's not hard to find a coot in these parts—just stop by any town café in the morning and there are usually a few at the counter talking about the weather and complaining about the good-for-nothin' local kids.

But there's another kind of coot: a mud hen. There are plenty of them around, too, when hunters aren't thinning them out. To be a good coot hunter, you need to practice at places like the Ashby Trap Range. To be sure you know what you're aiming for, the range has erected a 10-foot-tall coot beside the adjoining lake. It was built in 1991 by Steve Morgan for the Ashby Coot Feed.

Morgan chose concrete as his medium. In retrospect, it might have been a better idea to use fiberglass. The coot's flapping wings weigh so much they have to be propped up by a bulky metal frame, making it look as if the bird is wearing a back brace—not so great for photos. Then again, had it been made from something less durable, it might be riddled with hunters' buckshot. At least concrete deflects gunfire.

Coots Trap Range, Rte. 78, Ashby, MN 56309

No phone

Hours: Always visible

Cost: Free

Directions: Just northeast of the intersection of Rtes. 10 and 78, at Little Lake.

Battle Lake
Big Indian

As you might suspect, Battle Lake is named after a war fought near here. Chief Wenonga led his Ojibwe warriors to victory over the Dakota, but not by much. It was 1795, and Wenonga marched some 50 warriors into battle. Only a few Ojibwe survived, one of them being Wenonga, but all the Dakota were slaughtered. The body of water was named *Ish-quan-a-de-win-ing* by Native Americans, which translates roughly as "Where but few survived." Settlers eventually renamed it Battle Lake.

Today a 23-foot statue of Chief "The Vulture" Wenonga stands on the western shore of Battle Lake. The 1979 fiberglass statue has its right hand raised in greeting, while its left hand grips a stone-headed tomahawk. The town celebrates Wenonga Days each July.

Halverson Park, Rte. 78, Battle Lake, MN 56515

(888) 933-5253

Hours: Always visible

Cost: Free

www.battlelake-mn.com

Directions: On Rte. 78, just south of the intersection with Rte. 16 (Lakeshore Dr.).

Don't approach this statue from the rear.

Belgrade
World's Largest Crow

Belgrade needs a scarecrow—an *enormous* scarecrow. Why? It appears an 18-foot crow is building a nest of logs atop a rest-stop bathroom, and it plans on staying. Maybe this 3,000-pound black bird felt it could lay claim to this spot, seeing as how it's on the eastern shore of Crow Lake, not far from the Crow River. Locals have appeased the bird since it arrived in 1990 by dressing up the surrounding park, but there should be no illusion as to who's in charge here.

Route 71, Belgrade, MN 56312

No phone

Hours: Always visible

Cost: Free

Directions: South of town on Rte. 71, just south of Rte. 19.

Bemidji
Concordia Language Villages

Anyone who's ever had to learn a foreign language in a hurry can tell you that total immersion is the best strategy. Want to learn German? Dump yourself in the middle of a Bavarian village. Italian? Move to the Tuscan countryside. But here's the rub: it's tough to find a Tuscan villa in the North Woods, right?

Wrong. You just need to know where to look. The four European-styled mini towns of the Concordia Language Villages serve as the campus for 20 different language programs, including French, German, Norwegian, Spanish, Korean, Danish, Russian, Japanese, Finnish, Chinese, and French Voyageur. More languages are added each year. If you want to see these out-of-place structures you have three options: (1) enroll in a class, (2) visit in the summer during one of the villages' two International Days celebrations, or (3) call them to see if you can tag along on one of the school's occasional tours.

9500 Ruppstrasse NE, Bemidji, MN 56601

(800) 450-2214 or (218) 586-2214

Hours: Call ahead for a tour

Cost: $470/week

www.concordialanguagevillages.org

Directions: Six miles east of Rte. 21 on Rte. 20, follow the signs.

WHAT YOU WON'T FIND AT CONCORDIA . . .

Concordia's immersion program isn't the answer to everyone's language needs. Take, for example, the Klingon language. Relatively new, it was invented by Dr. Marc Okrand for the movie *Star Trek III: The Search for Spock*. Dozens of Trekkies have paid good money to learn the native tongue of this fake planet at a language camp run by Glen Proechel in nearby Red Lake Falls. Efforts are being made at the Interstellar Language School to translate the Bible into Klingon—as if it would do those evil, intergalactic warriors any good!

And for you out-of-staters who feel as if you've been dropped onto another planet, perhaps you should check out a copy of *How to Talk Minnesotan: A Visitor's Guide* by Howard Mohr (Penguin, 1987). It'll teach you the proper use and pronunciation of thousands of indigenous terms, such as "You bet," "Yep," and "Heckuva."

Fireplace of the States and Paul's Stuff

Moviegoers laughed at Lucille Ball when she collected rocks during her honeymoon journey in *The Long, Long Trailer*, but Desi was downright *hostile*. When he discovered the stones while driving up a mountain pass, he chucked them all off a precipice. Still, his attitude toward geographically significant rocks hasn't always been in vogue.

Take the case of the Fireplace of the States, a project started by local resident Harry E. Roese in the 1920s. He began collecting rocks on his travels, then brought them back with a plan to embed them in his resort's fireplace . . . a rock from Yellowstone . . . a dinosaur bone . . . gopher stones to make the letter *M*. . . . Wanting to complete his collection, Rose wrote to all of this nation's governors asking them to contribute a piece for the fireplace. Stones and bricks were ripped from the base of the Statue of Liberty, the U.S. Capitol, and lesser-known spots from each of the 48 states, plus several Canadian provinces. Under contract from the WPA, masons Charles Budge and Mark Morse constructed the fireplace between 1934 and 1935. Tourists came from all 48 states to see what they'd lost.

Sixty years later in 1995, when Bemidji's new tourist information center was built next to the Paul and Babe statues, the fireplace was moved to this location. In addition to the fireplace, you can see the world's largest collection of Paul Bunyan artifacts. Mounted on the wall and encased in glass cabinets, you'll find Bunyan's oversized broom, ax, Zippo lighter, CB radio, dice, playing cards, candleholder, fishing hook, potato masher, chocolate bar, cigar, toothpick, belt, wallet, class ring, nightcap, razor, toothpaste, fly swatter, toenail clippings (uck!), and underwear. (They're boxers.)

Bemidji Chamber of Commerce, 300 Bemidji Ave., PO Box 66, Bemidji, MN 56601
(800) 458-2223 or (218) 444-3541
E-mail: chamber@bemidji.org
Hours: September–May, Monday–Friday 9 A.M.–5 P.M.; June–August, Monday–Saturday
 9 A.M.–6 P.M.
Cost: Free
www.bemidji.org or www.visitbemidji.com
Directions: At the intersection of 3rd St. and Bemidji Ave. (Rte. 197).

BEMIDJI
Actress **Jane Russell** was born in Bemidji on June 21, 1921.

Lobo!

Stuffed and standing in a glass case in front of Morell's Trading Post in Bemidji is one of the mangiest, meanest, nastiest looking wolves you'd ever want to see, dead or alive. He is none other than Lobo, the smartest predator the North Woods ever saw. For 12 years, between 1926 and 1938, Lobo attacked three deer a week from Lake Itasca to Red Lake. That's 1,200 dead Bambis!

Lobo's success was a result of his unique strategy: he never returned to the scene of a kill, never traveled on trails, never took a mate, and never touched poison left for him. He also never attacked cattle or horses, or any other livestock for that matter. Still, some locals had it in for him (probably because the wolf consistently outwitted them). In 1936, Algot Wicken almost caught Lobo with a wire snare, but the wily wolf broke free. Two years later, Wicken finally captured the wolf with a foot trap. Lobo was still alive and growling, five days after having his leg crushed in the trap's teeth. Wicken shot him. It was then that he discovered the previous wire snare still wrapped around the creature's neck, embedded in its flesh.

The wolf's painful end led some to rethink their relentless pursuit of this predator that had done the citizenry no direct harm. After all, wasn't he just doing what wolves do? Those that wanted him dead and those who admired his skill agreed that his body should be put on display. The 140-pound, 3-foot-tall deer killer was mounted with his ears laid back and his teeth in a permanent snarl, just the way he would have wanted it.

Morell's Trading Post, 301 N. Bemidji Ave., Bemidji, MN 56601

(888) 667-3557 or (218) 751-4321

Hours: Always visible

Cost: Free

www.paulbunyan.net/users/jules

Directions: Just across the street from the Paul and Babe statues, at 3rd St.

BRECKENRIDGE

The mayor of Breckenridge held the record for the World's Longest Beard in 1935.

The second-most-photographed statues in the United States.

Paul and Babe

If you want somebody to thank or blame for all of Minnesota's oversized roadside attractions, start with these two statues in Bemidji. Both were built in 1937 for the town's Winter Carnival; Paul by Cyril Dickenson (using Mayor Earl Bucklen as a model, a man who apparently had a disproportionately small head), and Babe by Jim Payton. The 18-foot Paul was erected by the lake, but the 8-foot-tall, 10-foot-long blue ox statue was mounted on a Model A Ford chassis so it could be pulled through town. What's more, Babe was rigged to blow smoke out of its nostrils.

Babe was such a hit that it toured the nation, even appearing in *Life* magazine. It returned to Bemidji in 1939, at which point it was fitted with car headlight eyeballs and cemented to the ground in a park beside Paul.

Soon other Minnesota communities developed severe cases of statue envy and began erecting their own oversize monuments. Worried that Paul and Babe might be forgotten in the fiberglass rush, the town gathered or constructed some of Paul's personal effects—for example, his three-barrel shotgun and gigantic telephone. The gun was later determined to be too violent, and it was removed. Paul's stature also grew; the outer "shell" was enlarged three times, but this only added to the puny-head problem.

Bemidji Ave. & 3rd St., Bemidji, MN 56601

(800) 458-2223 or (218) 444-3541

Hours: Always visible

Cost: Free

www.bemidji.org/kids.htm or www.paulbunyan.net/bemidji/chamber/index.html

Directions: On Rte. 197 (Bemidji Ave.), on the southwest shore of Lake Bemidji.

ANOTHER BEMIDJI BIG GUY

In 1952 another oversized statue was built in town, this one in Library Park, three blocks north of Paul and Babe: Chief Shay-Now-Ish-Kung, better known as Chief Bemidji. (Please don't confuse him with the fiberglass "Injun Joe" statue across the street at Morell's.) He was created by Eric Boe from concrete, and was meant to be an eight-foot reminder as to who lived here *first*, and it wasn't some tree-choppin' lumberjack. The area's early settlers misnamed the real chief because they didn't listen to their own question. The exchange went something like this: "What do you call this lake, Chief?" they asked Shay-Now-Ish-Kung. "Bemidji," he replied. "Oh, pleased to meet you, Chief Bemidji! Mind if we name this lake after you?" Shay-Now-Ish-Kung rolled his eyes and never corrected them.

CROOKSTON

Residents of Crookston may not listen to political stump speeches and eat popcorn at the same time.

Oxen do not recall this era fondly.

Crookston
World's Largest Ox Carts

Many of the early settlers in the northern plains arrived by way of the Pembina Trail, which ran from St. Paul, Minnesota to Winnipeg, Canada. The transportation of choice was the oxcart, a simple two-wheeled rickshaw-like contraption. It wasn't as classy as a covered wagon but it got the job done.

There are two oversized oxcarts in Crookston today, a town located along the old Pembina Trail and that celebrates Ox Cart Days in mid-August every year. The first cart stands 15 feet tall outside the Red River Valley Shows exhibit hall on the north end of town. It was built out of concrete by Ernie Konikson in 1965 and features an ox and a bearded settler walking behind it. The Polk County Museum on the southeast side of town has the other, though it has neither an ox nor a driver. Combined, these carts could have moved the contents of the first settlement.

Red River Valley Shows, Fisher & University Aves., Crookston, MN 56716

(218) 281-8053

Hours: Always visible

Cost: Free

Directions: One block north of Rte. 61/11 (Fisher Ave.) on Rte. 2/75 (University Ave.) on the west frontage road.

Polk County Pioneer Museum, 719 E. Robert St., Crookston, MN 56716

(800) 809-5997 or (218) 281-1038

Hours: Always visible

Cost: Free

www.crookston.net/museum/default.htm

Directions: On the south end of Rte. 2 (Robert St.).

FERGUS FALLS

Fifty-nine Fergus Falls–area residents were killed during a windstorm on June 22, 1919.

The Fergus Falls City Hall (112 W. Washington Avenue), built in 1928, is a replica of Independence Hall in Philadelphia.

Ride 'em Otterboy! Photo by Jim Frost

Fergus Falls
World's Largest Otter

Otters are slippery critters, but that's not the reason it's so difficult to get atop the otter in a Fergus Falls park . . . it's because its so huge. But if you're lucky on your visit, some local kids will have pulled a picnic table over to the statue to make it easy to vault onto its back for a photo. If you want to play it safe, bring a ladder.

The World's Largest Otter was built near the shore of Grotto Lake by Robert Bruns to honor Otter Tail County—Fergus Falls is the county seat. The otter is 40 feet long from its black nose to its rump. Its tail curls around to the front, forming a makeshift slide. The whole thing is made of heavy-duty concrete. Because it is so sturdy, nobody complains if you climb onto it for a photo shoot.

Adams Park, Vernon Ave. & Concord St., Fergus Falls, MN 56537

(800) 726-8959 or (218) 739-0125

Hours: Always visible

Cost: Free

www.fergusfalls.com

Directions: Three blocks north of Rte. 210 on Pebble Lake Rd. (which turns into Vernon Ave.).

Gargantuan gobbler.

Frazee
World's Largest Turkey

With the possible exception of Benjamin Franklin (who wanted the turkey to be the national bird), Americans have had it in for gobblers. If we see a turkey at all, it's plucked, roasted, and stuffed with bread crumbs on

Thanksgiving. But in Frazee, where much of the local economy depends on the birds, one turkey has a place of honor: Big Tom. He stands 22 feet tall and watches over the population from a hill outside town. (There's a smaller, 7-foot turkey downtown at the intersection of Routes 10 and 87.)

He is not, however, the first Big Tom in Frazee. The original fiberglass statue survived only 12 years before it went up in flames on July 1, 1998. No, he was not roasted in a midsummer feast; maintenance crews accidentally hit him with a blowtorch and, within minutes, out popped the World's Largest Meat Thermometer. Well done! Apparently, fiberglass is much more flammable than turkey meat. A new Big Tom arrived by September.

Lions Park, Rtes. 29 & 10, Frazee, MN 56544

No phone

Hours: Always visible

Cost: Free

www.2havefun.com/Places/North-West/Frazee/

Directions: On the south side of town, by the dam, just south of the lakes.

Hackensack
Paul Bunyan's Sweetheart

If you always wondered if Babe the Blue Ox was Paul Bunyan's true love, you need to do two things: (1) stop watching Jerry Springer and (2) take a trip to Hackensack. LucetteDiana Kensack stands on the shores of Birch Lake, all 17 feet of her. A sign proclaims her to be Paul's girlfriend, but there are hints she's much more. She wears a wedding band, and the town claims to have a wedding license taken out by her and Paul. And then there's the human-sized Paul Junior standing by her side.

Now there's nothing to say the pair had to be married to produce this child. Every indication is that LucetteDiana is a liberated woman, retaining her full name despite the town's paperwork. Whether or not Paul Junior was born out of wedlock, you should probably think twice about calling him a bastard.

LucetteDiana Kensack was built in 1952 by Doad Schroeder, a local grocer. Her striped dress billows out toward the lake, and has a trapdoor for easy entry. ("To make repairs," Schroeder claimed.) She had a makeover in 1991 after a freak windstorm blew her head off. The new noggin is a definite improvement.

Lake Ave. & Birch St., PO Box 373, Hackensack, MN 56452

(800) 279-6135 or (218) 675-6135

Hours: Always visible

Cost: Free

www.hackensackchamber.com

Directions: On the east shores of Birch Lake, two blocks west of Rte. 371.

LucetteDiana and her little bastard.

Something fishy killed Paul.

Kelliher
Paul Bunyan's Grave

Sorry to be the one to break the news if you haven't already heard, but Paul Bunyan has long since gone to that Big Logging Camp in the Sky. You'd think he'd have been buried in the World's Largest Open-Pit Mine, but you'd be mistaken—he was buried in the little town of Kelliher.

There's not much to see but a tombstone over a 40-foot-long mound in a city park. His epitaph?

Paul Bunyan
Born 1794
Died 1899
Here Lies Paul, And That's All

How did the guy expire? A "modern Chippewa legend" says the mighty warrior Nanabojo was responsible. After watching Bunyan lay waste to forests across North America, Nanabojo decided the giant had to be stopped, so he whacked Bunyan to a pulp with a large fish. Was it a case of ecological self-defense, or was it murder? You decide.

1st St. & Rte. 72, Kelliher, MN 56650
No phone
Hours: Always visible
Cost: Free
Directions: Just south of Rte. 103 on Clark Ave. (Rte. 72).

Lake Itasca
Birthplace of the Mississippi River

Everyone's got to start somewhere, and the same goes for rivers. America's biggest, the Mighty Mississippi, begins its 2,552-mile journey as little more than a trickle running out of Lake Itasca. Up here it's known as the Mite-y Mississippi, and you can walk across the river on stepping stones. (A popular tourist T-shirt brags, "I walked across the Mississippi!")

Henry Schoolcroft is credited with finding the origin of the Mississippi in 1832, but in truth he'd been led there by a native Ojibwe named Ozawindib. Schoolcroft dusted off his Latin to name this lake, which is a combination of ver*itas* ("true") and *ca*put ("head").

Itasca State Park, HC05 Box 4, Lake Itasca, MN 56460
(218) 266-2110
Hours: Always visible
Cost: $4/car
www.dnr.state.mn.us/state_parks/itasca/index.html or www.itascaarea.com
Directions: Headwaters just south of the intersection of Rtes. 2 and 200, at the park's north entrance.

Long Prairie
Beer Can Aliens

On October 23, 1965, James Townsend was driving down a country road toward Long Prairie when he ran across a 35-foot-high rocket-shaped craft. It was hard to miss—it was parked in the middle of the gosh-durn road!! He thought of ramming the rocket to disable it for "evidence," but his truck had died. After he coasted to a stop, three creatures that looked like . . . well . . . like walking beer cans . . . came out and started *watching* Townsend. After a few minutes, the six-inch aliens returned to their UFO and shot off into space.

Authorities dismissed Townsend's beer-can Martians as the rantings of a man who'd had too many cans of beer, but several raccoon hunters backed up his story of a bright light blasting off toward the horizon. When news got around, a highway crew rushed out to replace asphalt on the stretch of Route 27 where the incident took place. Sounds suspicious to me.

Route 27, Long Prairie, MN 56347

No phone

Hours: Late at night

Cost: Free

Directions: Four miles from town on Rte. 27, heading toward Little Falls.

LONG PRAIRIE
Long Prairie claims to be the Largest Little Piggie Market.

MAINE
Supreme Court **Justice William O. Douglas** was born in Maine on October 16, 1898.

MARGIE
A reddish Bigfoot was seen sitting in a swamp near Margie in November 1978.

That's a heckuva grasshopper!

Menahga
St. Urho Statue
Here's a story: long ago in Europe, a country was overrun with a plague of pests, so a brave fellow stepped forward to drive the vermin from the land.

For his courage, the exterminator was made a saint. Was it St. Patrick? Nooooooo . . . St. Urho! Using only the booming sound of his voice chanting, "Heinasirkka, Heinasirkka, menetaala hiiteen!" ("Grasshopper, grasshopper, go to hell!"), St. Urho drove all the grasshoppers out of Finland and saved the grape crop.

Is it just a coincidence that nobody ever heard of this fellow before the 1950s? Or that his official Saint Day was assigned to be March 16, the day before St. Pat's? Or that the Finns celebrate the expulsion of grasshoppers by dressing in royal purple and Nile green, and drinking bucketsful of wine and grape juice on this holiest of Finnish days? Naaaah. A local paper claimed Urho was "just as authentic as the Jolly Green Giant."

Menahga Finns have gone a step further to honor their beloved St. Urho: in 1982 they erected a chainsaw sculpture of the saint holding a two-foot-long grasshopper impaled on a pitchfork. Unfortunately, this St. Urho was not as frightening to termites or Mother Nature as the original had been to grasshoppers, and the statue began to deteriorate. He was replaced with a fiberglass model, and the original statue was moved to a mausoleum in a local cemetery.

Helsinki Blvd. & Rte. 71, Menahga, MN 56464

No phone

Hours: Always visible

Cost: Free

www.geocities.com/Heartland/Fields/8516/urho.html

Directions: At the south end of town at Third St. SE.

Moorhead
A Prairie Home Cemetery

Fans of Garrison Keillor's *A Prairie Home Companion* probably know— but not *all* of them do—that Lake Wobegon is a fictitious Minnesota everytown. Fewer, though, know the radio show's name comes from a small cemetery in the middle of Moorhead.

The Prairie Home Cemetery is about as plain a cemetery as the simple folks buried there—not a lot of statuary, and many of the tombstones are embedded into the ground for easy mowing. In fact, there's nothing to suggest that it was ever the inspiration for a multimillion-dollar media sensation. But it was.

Rte. 75 & 8th Ave. S, Moorhead, MN 56560

No phone

Hours: Daily 7 A.M.–6 P.M.

Cost: Free

www.rootsweb.com/~mnclay/prairiehome.htm

Directions: Three blocks west of the Moorhead State University campus on S. 8th St.
(Rte. 75) at 8th Ave. S.

MORE WOBEGON WONDERS?

Since Lake Wobegon doesn't really exist, many places have laid claim to the town's inspiration. First on the list is Anoka, a suburb of the Twin Cities. Keillor grew up in Anoka and attended Anoka High School (3939 Seventh Avenue) from 1956 to 1960, though his family's home was in nearby Brooklyn Park (200 Brookdale Drive). In his senior year, he was a member of the Young Republicans. That would change when he went away to college.

After leaving the University of Minnesota, Keillor moved with his first wife to Freeport, another town that claims to be a model for Lake Wobegon. The couple moved there so Keillor could join the staff of KSJR at St. John's University in Collegeville, where he worked on *The Morning Program*. You can still get a cup of coffee at Charlie's Café (115 Main Street E) which many people argue is the inspiration for the current show's Chatterbox Café.

Another burg claiming the Lake Wobegon mantle is Marine on St. Croix on the state's eastern border. Keillor's Ralph's Pretty Good Grocery is said to be based on the general store in town, once owned by a guy named Ralph. Keillor lived in Marine St. Croix after he went to work for KSJN in St. Paul. The flagship station of Minnesota Public Radio was the first place Keillor began making up commercials for fictitious sponsors to inject between classical music. Those commercials became the basis for *A Prairie Home Companion*.

Goodie, goodie gumdrops!

Nevis
Gingerbread Day Care

If you named your children Hansel and Gretel (and why would you do such a thing?!?), you might want to warn them before enrolling them at the classiest day-care facility in Nevis, especially if the kids are a little chunky. Otherwise, you might have your hands full dragging them out of the SUV on the first day you drop them off.

You see, the building that houses Cookie's Day Care has been painted to resemble a gingerbread house, complete with icing on the eaves, candy-cane pillars, and a toy soldier standing guard. And if you've fed your children healthy doses of Grimm's fairy tales (and why would you do such a thing?!?), they just might think you're plumping them up . . . for dinner!!!

Cookie's Day Care, 119 Bunyan Trails Dr., Nevis, MN 56467

(218) 652-2400

Hours: Always visible

Cost: Free

Directions: On Rte. 2 (Bunyan Trails Dr.), across the street from the World's Largest Tiger Muskie.

The 747 of insects.

Ottertail
World's Largest Dragonfly

Unlike so many of this state's gigantic statues, the World's Largest Dragonfly was built to be moved. In fact, it is the goodwill ambassador for the International Center for Dragonfly Culture, an organization "to promote awareness that a healthy food chain is essential to the lake country environment." The dragonfly was constructed in 2000 by high school senior Marty Sazama and his uncle, Bill Wenner, for Grass Roots, a retail outlet for bedding plants and eco-friendly gifts.

The folks at Grass Roots will gladly cart the giant bug to your local celebration, as long as the event promotes wildlife, clean water, responsible outdoor activities—that sort of thing. Tractor pulls and monster truck rallies need not apply. And what if you do host one of those nasty get-togethers? This 30-foot carnivorous insect will come to life, swoop in on your pollution party, and devour all the litterbugs. The choice is yours.

Grass Roots Plants & Gifts, 212 N. Highway 78, Ottertail, MN 56571

(218) 367-2503

Hours: Always visible

Cost: Free

www.grassrootsmnusa.com/ICDFC/default.htm

Directions: Southwest of Ottertail along Rte. 78.

Pelican Rapids
Minnesota Minnie

A few years ago (geologically speaking), a 15-year-old female drowned in Lake Pelican. Her skeleton was discovered along with a dagger and a conch shell. Had she waded into the water after the shell, or was there some sort of foul play involving the dagger? It was rather hard to tell—her bones weren't recovered until 10,000 years after she died, give or take 1,000 years, long after the glacial lake had dried up. It was 1931, and a road crew was widening Route 59 north of Pelican Rapids when they unearthed the evidence. Archaeologists dubbed the bones Minnesota Man. Later her sex was determined, and she was renamed Minnesota Minnie.

Hers turned out to be some of the oldest human remains ever uncovered in North America, but you'll never see them. Though the skeleton's features suggested Minnie was not of Native American stock, they were turned over to the Sioux nation and reburied in South Dakota. Is that the end of the story? Pretty much. A stone monument was erected on the site, but her likely killers got away scot-free!

Route 59, Pelican Rapids, MN 56572

No phone

Hours: Always visible

Cost: Free

Directions: Three miles north of town on Rte. 59, just north of the Rte. 4 intersection.

MOORHEAD

Moorhead was named the Wickedest City in the World in the late 19th century.

Polar explorer **Roald Amundsen** had two teeth extracted when in Moorhead to lecture at Concordia College. The teeth, still in the possession of the school, are all that remain of Amundsen. The rest of him was lost near the North Pole in 1928, along with his plane, while searching for survivors of a downed airship.

Pelican + Rapids = Pelican Rapids.

World's Largest Pelican

For years, Pelican Rapids had a concrete spillway on Mill Pond Dam at the headwaters of the Pelican River in the center of town, but it didn't have a pelican. The question loomed: how would tourists know they were in Pelican Rapids without a pelican beside the rapids?

The solution came in 1957 when local boosters Anton and Ted Resset built a 15.5-foot pelican out of rebar and concrete, and placed it beside the river. With the exception of an occasional paint job, the big-billed bird has survived the elements well . . . better than most *real* pelicans, which are in short supply in this town. If you're into *fake* pelicans, there's another, made of fiberglass, outside the Pelican Motel (900 N. Broadway) on the north side of town.

Pelican Rapids honors local birds each July with a town festival. Pelican Days? Nope—the annual Turkey Festival. After all, who wants to eat pelican?

Broadway & W. Mill St., Pelican Rapids, MN 56572

(800) 545-3711

Hours: Always visible

Cost: Free

Directions: Just east of Rte. 59 (Broadway) at the Mill Pond dam, next to the post office.

Could Blackduck be any more literal?

MONUMENTS OF THE OBVIOUS

If Minnesotans are nothing else, they're straightforward and literal. Pelican Rapids isn't the only town with public sculpture honoring its name:

★ A nine-foot fiberglass moose stands at the intersection of Routes 61 and 10 in **Moose Lake**, next to the town's Tourist Information Center. (www.mooselake-mn.com/home.htm)

★ The town of **Grey Eagle** was named for a gray eagle shot by A. M. Crowell here in 1868. Since that creature is long gone, a more permanent eagle (106 State Street) was carved in 1985 from a dead tree with a chainsaw by artist Larry Jensen. He then painted it gray.

★ **Deerwood** has an eight-foot fiberglass buck jumping over a log on its main drag (Maple Road East and Front Street). Just to be clear, the town isn't called Bucklog; it's Deerwood.

MORE MONUMENTS OF THE OBVIOUS

★ **Starbuck** uses a similar buck statue (7th and Main Streets), this one made out of concrete, but it has a star hanging between its antlers. Star. Buck. Get it? (www.starbuckminnesota.net)

★ **Blackduck** has no fewer than *three* big black ducks around town. The first quacker was erected in 1938 by P. J. St. Amant. It was mounted on a sled that could be pulled through the town during the winter, ridden by the Blackduck Queen, of course. The 18-foot, cement-and-wood bird has since been mounted on a pedestal (Route 47 and Margaret Avenue). The second black duck didn't arrive until 1972, and it was a puny variation on the first. Becky Balsiger Foley made the five-foot-long statue out of papier-mâché for the Drake Motel (172 Pine Avenue SW).

The most recent incarnation of the town's namesake is more active than its ancestors, flapping its wings as it prepares to take off . . . or is it coming in for a landing? It's made of fiberglass. (Heritage Park, Summit Avenue and Frontage Road). As you might expect, Blackduck celebrates Duck Days each July. (www.webwinder.com/blackduck/ bldkhome.html)

NEW YORK MILLS

New York Mills hosts the annual Great American Think-Off each June (www.think-off.org). Local philosophers tackle life's great unanswered questions, such as "How many roads must a man walk down?" and "Which came first, the chicken or the egg?" The winner receives a trophy of Rodin's *Thinker* seated on a tractor.

OSAKIS

While traveling from Osakis and Eagle Bend on May 10, 1961, Richard Vogt's car was hit by a curious "ball of fog." When the car was blasted by the cloud, the interior became unbearably hot, and Vogt had to pull over. It was then that he discovered his rooftop had been burned.

OTTER TAIL COUNTY

Otter Tail County has more lakes than any other in Minnesota: 1,048.

Geeeeeeez—that smarts!

Rothsay
World's Largest Prairie Chicken

Unlike so many static monuments, this four-and-a-half-ton cement masterpiece is caught in an action pose, bent over, pecking and scratching and puffing up its bright orange air sacs. It is exhibiting the bird's unique mating ritual, called booming. If you angle your camera just right, it'll look like you're under attack. Yeeeeeooooowwww!!!!

The statue was built in 1976 by local sculptors Art Fosse and Dale

Western. Rothsay had named itself the Prairie Chicken Capital of Minnesota a year earlier, and it seemed like the right thing to do. The statue is 13 feet tall and 18 feet from tip to tail.

I-94 & Rte. 52, Rothsay, MN 56579

No phone

Hours: Always visible

Cost: Free

Directions: Just south of I-94.

Sauk Centre
Aliens Attack!

On October 8, 1984, Robert and Jackie Bair screeched into the Truckers Inn, raving that their 18-wheeler was under attack. They calmed down just enough to tell the skeptical crowd that they had accidentally rammed a peanut-shaped spacecraft near Billings, Montana, and had been trying to outrun the angry Martians ever since. The aliens were about eight inches high, looked like birds with human feet, and had V-shaped heads. What's more, they fired metal shavings at the couple, diving and bombing their cab from above.

There was little time to talk, the pair warned, for the aliens were perched outside at that very moment on the telephone lines and in the treetops. A crowd from the diner went out to the parking lot to investigate but found nothing. The Bairs chose to drive on, still seeing something that everyone else didn't. The local newspaper investigated, but they didn't find anything, either.

But is that just part of the Martians' plan?

Truckers Inn, I-94 & Rte. 71, Sauk Centre, MN 56378

(320) 352-5241

Hours: Always open

Cost: Free

Directions: I-94 at Rte. 71.

Sinclair Lewis's Main Street

If you want to piss off your hometown, author Sinclair Lewis could give you a few pointers. First, write a scathing exposé of small-town life, fill it with small-minded folks, and be sure to only thinly disguise your characters' identities. In the process, draw worldwide attention to your former neighbors' personal shortcomings. Go on to win the Pulitzer Prize and the Nobel Prize for Literature, flit around in artistic social circles, then return home only when nobody can tell you off to your face ... because you're in an urn. Is it any wonder that *Main Street*, Sinclair's classic work of American literature, wasn't taught in the Sauk Centre schools until the mid-1960s?

(Harry) Sinclair Lewis was born in Sauk Centre on February 7, 1885, in a building across the street from his eventual boyhood home. The birthplace at 811 Third Street South (today known as Sinclair Lewis Avenue) was torn down years ago. A new home stands in its place, but his boyhood home is still there and open to visitors. Lewis lived there from 1889 to 1903; the building still contains some of the family heirlooms, including Sinclair's bed and a white sugar bowl brought over by one of Lewis's ancestors on the *Mayflower*.

Boyhood Home, 810 Sinclair Lewis Ave., PO Box 222, Sauk Centre, MN 56378
(320) 352-6119
Hours: June–August, Monday–Friday 9:30 A.M.–5 P.M.; October–April, Monday–Friday 8:30 A.M.–2 P.M.
Cost: Adults $3, Seniors (62+) $2.50, Kids (6–10) $1.50
Directions: Three blocks west of Rte. 71 (Main St.) on Rte. 17 (Sinclair Lewis Ave.).

Lewis's father was a physician; his mother died of tuberculosis when he was five. His father took Isabel Warner as his second wife. She encouraged Sinclair to read literature and write. In high school, Lewis worked as the night clerk at the Palmer House Hotel (228 Main Street), but was fired two weeks later for reading on the job and being a general scatterbrain.

But Lewis got the last laugh in 1920 when *Main Street* was published and the Palmer House was skewered as the Minniemashie House in Gopher Prairie, Lewis's new name for Sauk Centre. In the novel, newlywed heroine Carol Kennicott arrives from St. Paul and unsuccessfully attempts to improve the cultural level of the town's pigheaded populace.

Lewis returned to Sauk Centre in 1951 after dying in Rome. His ashes were interred in the family plot in Greenwood Cemetery. The town slowly forgave, and then embraced, its prodigal native son. It celebrates Sinclair Lewis Days in mid-July each year and has opened a Sinclair Lewis Interpretive Center just off the interstate.

Sinclair Lewis Interpretive Center, Rte. 71 & I-94, Sauk Centre, MN 56378

(612) 352-5201

Hours: May–September, Monday–Friday 8:30 A.M.–3 P.M.

Cost: Free

www.saukcentre.com

Directions: At the intersection of Rte. 71 and I-94.

Postmaster Krueger must have been a loon.

Vergas
World's Largest Loon

The folks of Vergas must have thought very highly of their former post-master, Ewald C. Krueger. While some towns name a park or a library or a road after a prominent citizen, Vergas erected a statue in his honor in 1963. Not a statue of Krueger, mind you, but a 20-foot concrete loon. It was commissioned by the local fire department and constructed by Robert Bruns, the same fellow who made the giant mallard in Wheaton. (Bruns's talents weren't limited to birds; he also did the oversized otter in nearby Fergus Falls.)

Folks who still remember Krueger are hard to come by in Vergas, the Home of the Loon. No doubt there will come a day when Krueger will only be known as the loon by the lake, and for all we know, that'll be just fine with him.

City Park, Rte. 4, Vergas, MN 56587

No phone

Hours: Always visible

Cost: Free

www.vergasmn.com

Directions: Just north of town, on the western tip of Long Lake, just west of the Rte. 228
  intersection.

PILLAGER
The town of Pillager was named for a trader who was robbed on the Crow Wing River.

STARBUCK
An eight-foot fiberglass hobo guards the Hobo Park Campground (101 S. Main Street) in Starbuck. The campground is located on the former site of a hobo camp that formed on the shores of Lake Minnewaska during the Great Depression.

STEPHEN
Deputy sheriff Val Johnson was attacked by a fireball while driving on Route 220 about 10 miles west of Stephen on August 27, 1979. The fireball smashed out one of his headlights and caused Johnson to pass out. Both Johnson's watch and the car's clock mysteriously lost 14 minutes.

TENSTRIKE
Tenstrike was named for the bowling term for a perfect frame.

A Starbucks nightmare.

Vining
Don't Cry over Spilt Coffee

Are you looking for a break from Minnesota's hyperliteral public sculpture? Come to Vining if you're looking for the abstract. You'll find the state's most recent additions to the artistic landscape to be a little more off the wall: a colossal clothespin . . . a supersized square knot . . . a titanic toe. . . .

They're the works of Ken Nyberg, who builds his creations out of scrap metal he collects from his job as a construction worker at grain elevators and farm buildings. Most of his pieces are located on the east end of town, next to the Bigfoot Gas and Grocery. There's a giant cup of coffee suspended in midair, its contents pouring onto the soil; a pair of pliers poised to crush a yard-long cockroach; and an Apollo astronaut planting a flag. (The latter is a tribute to his daughter, Karen L. Nyberg, an astronaut candidate at the Johnson Space Center.)

Nyberg's home and studio are located a mile north of town, and he doesn't seem to be running out of ideas or energy. Expect something new, bizarre, and perhaps disturbing on your next visit. Nyberg has even more sculptures along Route 10 in nearby New York Mills.

Rte. 210, PO Box 141, Vining, MN 56588

No phone

Hours: Always visible

Cost: Free

Directions: Scattered all along Rte. 210.

WADENA

A 14-foot ice cream cone stands outside Down Home Foods (636 Jefferson Street N) in Wadena. It was built of concrete in 1973 by Chuck Sartell.

WENDELL

Lightning Lake, north of Wendell, was named for a man killed by lightning on its shores.

King Quacker in the Land of the Ducks.

Wheaton
World's Largest Mallard

If you're a nearsighted hunter, stay away from Wheaton—you're an accident waiting to happen. Though you may not be able to hit the broad side

of a barn, much less a duck, you'd have no problem drawing a bead on one duck in town: the World's Largest Mallard. But should you fire on this easy target, you're more likely to be arrested for damaging public property or, worse yet, you might get hit by ricocheting buckshot. You see, this bird's made of concrete.

The statue to the favorite local quarry was erected in 1959 by Robert Bruns. It's 26 feet tall and appears to be taking flight out of a stand of cattails. Bruns designed the statue using "a paperweight, a Grain Belt Beer ad, and a dime store statue" as models.

500 S. Rte. 75, Wheaton, MN 56296

No phone

Hours: Always visible

Cost: Free

www.cityofwheaton.com/welcome.htm

Directions: Two blocks south of Rte. 27 on Rte. 75.

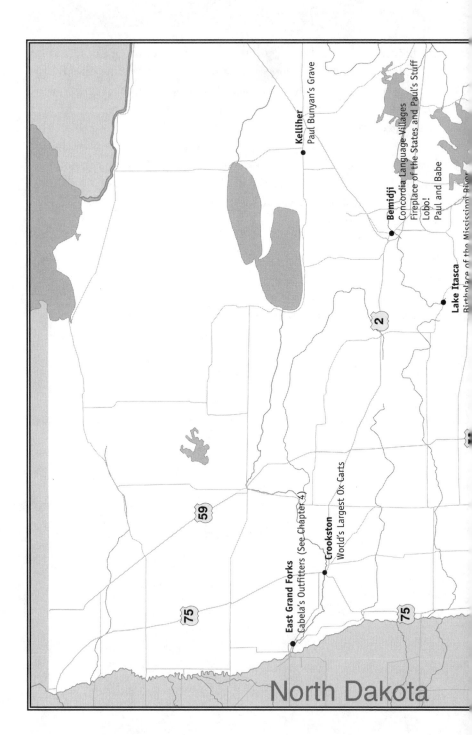

Kelliher
Paul Bunyan's Grave

Bemidji
Concordia Language Villages
Fireplace of the States and Paul's Stuff
Lobo!
Paul and Babe

Lake Itasca
Birthplace of the Mississippi River

2

59

75

East Grand Forks
Cabela's Outfitters (See Chapter 4)

Crookston
World's Largest Ox Carts

75

North Dakota

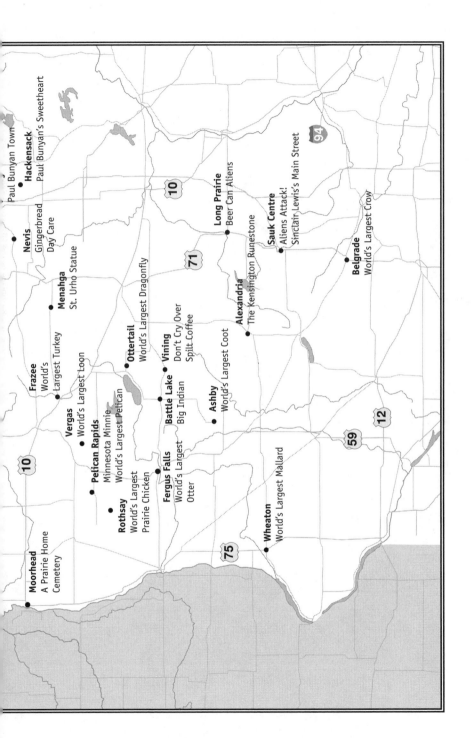

Paul Bunyan Town

Hackensack
Paul Bunyan's Sweetheart

Nevis
Gingerbread
Day Care

Menahga
St. Urho Statue

Frazee
World's
Largest Turkey

Vergas
World's Largest Loon

Pelican Rapids
Minnesota Minnie
World's Largest Pelican

Ottertail
World's Largest Dragonfly

Vining
Don't Cry Over
Spilt Coffee

Battle Lake
Big Indian

Ashby
World's Largest Coot

Long Prairie
Beer Can Aliens

Sauk Centre
Aliens Attack!
Sinclair Lewis's Main Street

Alexandria
The Kensington Runestone

Belgrade
World's Largest Crow

Rothsay
World's Largest
Prairie Chicken

Fergus Falls
World's Largest
Otter

Moorhead
A Prairie Home
Cemetery

Wheaton
World's Largest Mallard

10

71

94

10

12

59

75

THE NOrtHEast

*M*innesota's northeast corner, often called the Arrowhead, is known for its mountain ranges, though truth be known, the open-pit mines that go *down* are more impressive than the iron ranges that go *up*. The region is popular with residents fleeing the Twin Cities on weekends, most of them looking to get away from it all.

But in the relentless pursuit of nature, many no doubt miss the human-made wonders all around them. Would folks be able to fish on Lake Ore-Be-Gone near Virginia if somebody hadn't removed the ore in the first place? Would anyone know just how cold International Falls could get without the two-story thermometer in a town park? Would the foliage be as pretty had the Virgin Mary not wiped out the plague of locusts years ago (as memorialized in a Cold Spring chapel)? No, no, most definitely no.

Enjoy these artificial attractions while you can—they may not last forever.

He's a talking lumberjack, and he's OK.
Photo by author, courtesy of the Paul Bunyan Amusement Center

Brainerd
World's Largest Talking Paul Bunyan

It may not be the state's oldest Paul Bunyan, but it's the only one that talks! Even better, Paul's voice isn't a tape on an endless loop, but he actually *looks* in your direction and addresses you by name! North

Woods magic? No, just some teenager in a control booth being fed information by your parents and friends.

The statue was built in 1949 by the Chicago & Northwestern Railroad as a promotional gimmick and is supposedly the World's Largest Talking Man. The statue was designed to resemble the Lincoln Memorial. It was sold a year after it was built to Sherman Levis and Ray Kuemichel for use as the centerpiece of Paul Bunyan Land. The statue is 26 feet tall (sitting), wears size 80 boots, and has 16-inch eyeballs that move back and forth.

Levis and Kuemichel acquired some of Bunyan's personal effects to display around their park as well, like his ax, telephone, harmonica, and post office box. A 15-foot-tall Babe the Blue Ox guards the park entrance. Inside the gates you'll find Henry, a squirrel the size of a kangaroo, and Sport, a dog cut in half in a sawmill accident. This unlucky pooch was sewed back together in time, but his back legs now point up rather than down. The mistake helps him run, since one pair can jog along while the other pair rests.

Paul Bunyan Land was renamed the Paul Bunyan Amusement Center and now has kiddie rides and a helicopter for adults who want to see Brainerd from the air. Scattered around the park are mechanical dioramas of mining camps and blacksmith shops that spring to life for a quarter. If you're not interested in the 19th or 20th centuries, try out the new Space Probe ride where a jet engine blows thrill seekers, inside a giant ball, up and down inside a vertical tube.

Paul Bunyan Amusement Center, PO Box 563, Brainerd, MN 56401
(218) 829-6342
Hours: May–September, daily 10 A.M.–7 P.M.
Cost: Adults $9.25, Seniors $4.50, Kids $9.25
www.paulbunyancenter.com
Directions: At the intersection of Rtes. 210 and 371, west of the Mississippi River Bridge.

AITKIN
A 12-foot-tall fiberglass blacksmith stands atop the Aikin Iron Works building (First Street and First Avenue NW).

Camp Ripley Junction
Hitler's Hanky and Cécile's Letters

As the Allied forces overran the Axis in Europe in 1944 and 1945, soldiers were known to pick up a war souvenir or two—and who can blame them? Three of these unique items are on display in this state military museum. The first, a handkerchief monogrammed with the initials AH, is none other than Hitler's hanky! It was liberated from his Munich apartment (on Prinzregentplatz) in May 1945. Beside it are two engraved shot glasses for Heinrich Himmler and for Eva Braun. The GI who got them also took their calling cards. Well, it's not like they were going to use them. . . .

Another popular display at the Minnesota Military Museum is a collection of letters sent by Cécile Cowdery to her husband Raymond from 1941 to 1945. Each envelope was covered in an elaborate color illustration. Scenes of Hitler getting his Axis kicked, Cécile in slinky negligées, and Raymond getting yelled at by officers were the most common images.

Minnesota Military Museum, 15000 Rte. 115, Camp Ripley Junction, MN 56345

(320) 632-7374

E-mail: mnmuseum@brainerd.net

Hours: May–August, Wednesday–Sunday 10 A.M.–5 P.M.; September–April, Thursday–
Friday 9 A.M.–4 P.M.

Cost: Suggested $2 donation

www.dma.state.mn.us/cpripley/SpecFeatures/muse1.htm

Directions: Seven miles north of Little Falls off Rte. 115, due north of the Main Gate.

AITKIN
The town of Aitkin was darkened unexpectedly on April 2, 1889, when the sun went black. It was not an eclipse, and it was never explained.

ARTHYDE
The town of Arthyde was named after the Hutchins brothers, Arthur and Clyde.

Center City
Drying Out the Stars

Where did Kitty Dukakis get shipped off to after she guzzled rubbing alcohol? Where did Matthew Perry end up (more than once)? Not the Betty Ford Clinic! Hazelton Rehabilitation Center was the first treatment center to define alcoholism as a disease, and they've been drying out stars for longer than that.

There have been others to visit Center City—actors Ben Vereen, Melanie Griffith, Sharon Gless, and Howard Rollins, Jr.; footballers Dexter Manley and Tommy Kramer—and quite a few more who have been able to keep their treatments secret. Hazelton will help anyone with a substance abuse problem, not just celebrities and has-beens. It's not cheap, but can you put a price on sharing a group encounter session with Andy Dick? I think not.

Hazelton Foundation, 15245 Pleasant Valley Rd., Center City, MN 55012
(651) 257-4010
Hours: Make an appointment
Cost: $4,500 for 28 days
Directions: Rte. 8 from I-35, east 14 miles, right on Pleasant Valley Rd., 200 yards.

BENA
The name of Lake Winnibigoshish, north of Bena, can be roughly translated from Ojibwe as "miserable, wretched, dirty water."

BRAINERD
The water tower in Brainerd is shaped like a medieval castle turret, complete with flags. Some call it Paul Bunyan's Flashlight.

All Brainerd men must, by law, grow beards.

BUHL
Buhl calls itself the Springs of Health and Pits of Wealth, referring to its natural springs and open-pit mines.

He could date the Statue of Liberty.

Chisholm
Iron Man Statue and Ironworld, USA

It's hard to miss the Iron Man Statue along Route 169. Atop a hill south of town, the 36-foot miner in a hard hat stands on a 55-foot pile of iron beams. Its official title is *The Emergence of Man Through Steel*, and it is the third-largest freestanding memorial in the United States—only the Statue of Liberty and the St. Louis Arch are larger.

You'd think such a stupendous monument to iron would be honor enough for the element (after all, is there a Tungston Man?), but just look across the highway and you'll see: Ironworld, USA! Situated on the edge of the Glen Open-Pit Mine, this interactive museum has something for everyone. For the kids, there's Pellet Pete's miniature golf course. Every hole is a different stage in the iron-mining process. As you would expect, the open-pit hole is the easiest. For the adults, a museum dangling over the mine's rim explains the process in further detail. For the old folks, there are replicas of a pioneer homestead, an Ojibwe tepee, and an old world Norwegian stabur house, each with a costumed docent to remind visitors how good the good old days were. It takes a lot of convincing.

Before you leave, be sure to take the train tour—two and a half miles around the circumference of the mine.

Ironworld, USA, Rte. 169, PO Box 392, Chisholm, MN 55719
(800) 372-6437 or (218) 254-7959
E-mail: marketing@ironworld.com
Hours: Statue always visible; Park open May–September, 9:30 A.M.–5 P.M.
Cost: Adults $8, Seniors (62+) $7, Kids (7–17) $6
www.ironworld.com
Directions: Just east of the Rte. 73 intersection, across from the McDonald's.

CASTLE DANGER
Castle Danger was named, somewhat belatedly, to warn a ship called the *Castle* that ran into the reefs just offshore.

Prairie-style petrol-pumper.

Cloquet
Frank's Fill-'er-Up

Frank Lloyd Wright was an architectural genius: Taliesin, Falling Water, the Guggenheim, and the Cloquet Gas 'n' Go.

Well, not exactly a Gas 'n' Go, but close. The Lindholm Service Station in Cloquet was built in 1956 for Ray Lindholm. It's the only Wright-designed gas station ever constructed. It was actually drawn up in 1932 as part of a never-realized working-class subdivision called Broadacre City. The community was to be filled with simple homes with attached carports, which Wright called Usonian, a vision of 1950s America two decades before it actually arrived.

Wright's design for the Lindholm Station was only partially completed. Rather than have ground-level pumps, he envisioned hoses hanging from the cantilevered canopy. The structure had a Jetsonesque second-floor waiting room where folks could watch the mechanics in action from above. But few people want to prolong their stay at a gas station these days, so the customer lounge is barely utilized, though the building is still used as a gas station.

202 Cloquet Ave., Cloquet, MN 55720

(218) 879-2279

Hours: Always visible

Cost: Free; Gas $1.33/gallon (unleaded), subject to change

Directions: At the intersection of Rtes. 45 (Cloquet Ave.) and 33.

CLOQUET

The town of Cloquet was engulfed in a forest fire on October 12, 1918, killing more than 500 residents.

Jessica Lange was born in Cloquet on April 20, 1949. She graduated from Cloquet High School in 1967 where, as a senior, she was a member of the Sno-Ball Committee.

COLD SPRING

Billy Carter's Billy Beer was brewed at the Cold Spring Brewing Company (now the Gluek Brewing Company).

CROSBY

Forty-one miners drowned when the Milford Mine north of Crosby flooded on February 5, 1924. Miners dug too close to Foley Lake (Route 6).

Bow down, bugs!!

Cold Spring
Grasshopper Chapel

While the Virgin Mary is not the official saint invoked against grasshopper plagues (that's either St. Dominic of Silos, or St. Tychon), she did seem to help out the folks of Minnesota in 1877—or so the story goes. Swarms of Rocky Mountain grasshoppers first invaded Minnesota's southern counties in 1874. Farmland was mowed clean as the insects returned each year until Governor John Pillsbury declared April 26, 1877, a statewide day of prayer. "Be gone, plague of locusts!" the faithful pleaded, and, remarkably, a freakish freezing rainstorm swept over the state and killed most of the eggs and infant insects.

Father Leo Winter saw the state's deliverance as a sign to start building, and before the summer's end a chapel was erected on this site. But while Mary may have helped out with the grasshoppers, she didn't do anything to stop the tornado that ripped through Cold Spring on June 28, 1894. The chapel was leveled, yet the Virgin's statue was salvaged.

A new chapel was constructed in 1952, this time out of granite. Over the main entrance is a bas-relief stone carving of two grasshoppers genuflecting at the feet of the Virgin Mary, who is ascending into heaven. They know who's boss.

Assumption Chapel, Chapel St. & Pilgrimage Rd., Cold Spring, MN 56320
(612) 685-3280
Hours: Always visible
Cost: Free
Directions: Just south of Rte. 23 at the east end of town.

Crosby
Nordic Inn Medieval B&B

Don't come to the Nordic Inn Medieval B&B expecting a silver tray with raspberry scones and cappuccino outside your door in the morning. More likely than not, you'll be sleeping off a bender and won't want to be bothered. That's because *B&B* here doesn't stand for "bed and breakfast," but "brew and bed." Guests are treated to an interactive-theater dinner, Viking style. They eat with their hands and wash it down with steins of beer. Actors in Viking garb drop by to plunder and pillage, comedically speaking. After they leave, you're free to take a dip in the hot tub in a fiberglass cave, but take off your chain mail—you don't want to sink!

Proprietor Rick Schmidthuber converted a 1909 church for this unique lodge, then changed his own name to Steinarr Elmerson, also known as the "Crazy Viking." Outside his establishment a chainsaw carving of Thor, god of thunder, guards the entrance. Four of the B&B's five rooms are old-Viking themed, with the beds placed in sailing skiffs. The final room has a new-Viking theme; it's called the Locker Room: astroturf carpet, lockers for closets, and goalposts for a headboard . . . to help you score. Don't forget to use the Green Bay Packers urinal.

210 First Ave. NW, Crosby, MN 56441
(218) 546-8299
E-mail: nordicbb@emily.net
Hours: Open year-round
Cost: $65–$125/night
www.vikinginn.com
Directions: Two blocks north of Rte. 210, two blocks east of Rte. 6.

Duluth
The Congdon Murders

The killer entered the 1905 mansion through the billiard room, beat night nurse to death with a candlestick holder, and smothered the wealthy dowager with a pink satin pillow. No, this wasn't a game of Clue, but a genuine pair of murders at Duluth's Glensheen Mansion on June 27, 1977. The victims? Heiress Elisabeth Congdon and her assistant, Velma Pietila. The suspect? Roger Caldwell, second husband of Congdon's adopted daughter Marjorie.

Though years earlier Marjorie had been set up with a generous living trust, it wasn't enough for the free-spending ne'er-do-well. So Marjorie talked her husband into offing the 83-year-old heiress to a multimillion-dollar mining fortune. Roger was sloppy—he was drunk at the time—and left a trail of evidence from Duluth to the Twin Cities, to the couple's home in Golden, Colorado. He was eventually convicted of the murders. Marjorie, on the other hand, was found not guilty a few years later. Because of conflicting information presented at Marjorie's trial, Roger was able to overturn his own conviction. Facing a new trial, he pleaded guilty to two counts of second-degree murder, and was released with time served.

Meanwhile, law enforcement officials still had their hands full with Marjorie. In 1983 she set fire to her home in Mound for insurance money. She was convicted of arson and fraud. Awaiting sentencing, she was picked up for shoplifting vitamins at a Byerley's in St. Louis Park. The judge sentenced her to two and a half years for starting the fire.

After serving one year, she was released and headed to Ajo, Arizona, to be with her third husband, Wally Hagen. When the couple had married in 1981, Marjorie had "forgotten" to divorce Roger Caldwell first, earning her a never-served criminal complaint for bigamy. (Roger Caldwell committed suicide in Latrobe, Pennsylvania, on May 17, 1988.) She was arrested for trying to burn down a neighbor's house with a gasoline-soaked rag placed on a windowsill, and was named as a suspect in 13 other suspicious fires in the area. Marjorie was found guilty of attempted arson in 1992, but before she was sentenced, begged the judge for one last day to get her affairs in order with Wally. She went home, and that night Wally died with a gas line open to his bedroom. Police found a suspicious suicide note that made it difficult to charge Marjorie with his murder. She is currently serving time, but she'll be released soon—so look out, future husband number four!

But back to Duluth. You won't hear about the infamous murders on the mansion's official tour; guides are trained to deflect all questions. For crime buffs, here's the scoop: the nurse's body was found on the windowseat between the first and second floors, on the lake side of the 39-room mansion. Elisabeth Congdon's bedroom was just to the right as you reach the top of those stairs.

Glensheen, 3300 London Rd., Duluth, MN 55804

(888) 454-GLEN or (218) 726-8910

Hours: May–October, daily 9:30 A.M.–4 P.M.; November–April, Saturday–Sunday, 11 A.M.–2 P.M.

Cost: Adults $8.75, Seniors (61+) $7, Teens (12–15) $7, Kids (6–11) $4

www.d.umn.edu/glen

Directions: On Rte. 61 (London Rd.), just north of 32nd Ave. E.

The Duluth Lynchings

If residents of northern states ever try to suggest that the American South was the only place where blatant racism led to mass violence, you might want to point out an incident that occurred in downtown Duluth on June 15, 1920. By most estimates, about one-tenth of this city's population participated in, or came to watch, the lynching of three African American men. The mob was reacting to reports that a group of workers from a traveling circus had raped a 17-year-old white woman in West Duluth the previous evening. The mob's actions would have been unjustified in any case, but the events become even more unsettling when you find out there was ample evidence *at the time* that no such rape ever occurred.

In all likelihood, the female "victim" and her white male companion had gone to the fields behind the circus tents for a sexual tryst in the high grass and were spotted (and perhaps embarrassed) by the black workers. The pair concocted a story that would spread through the town the next day: two workers held him at gunpoint while four others brutally raped her. But neither could identify a single perpetrator from a group of 40 men dragged from the circus train. Nevertheless, six men were held for questioning. An examining doctor concluded the female accuser showed no physical or psychological signs of ever having been attacked.

That didn't matter to the mob that built over the course of the next day. Around 8 P.M., a crowd of between five and ten thousand rioters descended on the Duluth City Jail (Superior Street and 2nd Avenue East) demanding the six detainees. At first the police officers tried to defend the station, but most stepped aside when they became overwhelmed. After the mob broke through the walls of several cells, three prisoners—Elias Clayton, Elmer Jackson, and Isaac McGhie—were dragged two blocks north and hung from a light post across from the Shrine Auditorium. A photographer snapped a commemorative shot of the mob and victims that was sold locally as a gruesome souvenir.

Only 19 rioters were ever charged with mob action, and only three of them were convicted. Nobody was ever charged with murder. A circus worker named Max Mason, however, was convicted of rape and sentenced to 30 years in prison. He was unexpectedly released four years later by a parole board. They never gave their reasons, though most felt it was an attempt to put the issue behind them . . . and under the rug.

Murder Site, First St. & Second Ave. E, Duluth, MN 55802

No phone

Hours: Always visible

Cost: Free

Directions: On the southwest corner.

Clayton/Jackson/McGhie Graves, Park Hill Cemetery, 2500 Vermillion Rd., Duluth, MN 55803

(218) 724-7149

Hours: Daily 9 A.M.–6 P.M.

Cost: Free

Directions: North on Jean Duluth Rd. from Arrowhead Rd., then west on Greenwood St. to Vermillion Rd.

Karpeles Library Museum

Not all of this nation's documents are held by the National Archives. Private collectors, like David Karpeles, have a good portion of them. Fortunately for us, Karpeles has a strong sense of historic and civic responsibility to accompany his private collector's mania. Rather than frame them to hang in his den, the real estate mogul has established several small museums across the United States where he can display the collection on a rotating basis. The Duluth branch of the Karpeles focuses on only 26 documents at a time, so you never know what you'll see when you visit.

The Karpeles collection includes the original draft of Lincoln's Emancipation Proclamation, George Washington's declaration making Thanksgiving a holiday, a draft of the Bill of Rights, a page from Noah Webster's original dictionary, Beethoven's *Emperor Concerto*, *Roget's Thesaurus*, Einstein's description of the theory of relativity, and the first draft of the Constitution of the Confederate States of America. It also has less important and less well-known items from the famous, such as Thomas Edison's gas bill (for $15.93), and a page from Isaac Newton's *The Ultimate Scientist and Religion*, in which he accuses priests of using "fake and tricky arguments."

902 E. First St., Duluth, MN 55805

(218) 728-0630

E-mail: kmuseumdul@aol.com

Hours: June–August, daily Noon–4 P.M.; September–May, Tuesday–Sunday Noon–
4 P.M.

Cost: Free

www.rain.org/~karpeles/dulfrm.html

Directions: One block west of Rte. 61 (London Rd.) at 9th Ave. E.

One BIG Ship

When the Iron Range's ore was being scraped out in the 1900s, the most efficient way to get it to the mills dotting the shores of the Great Lakes was by ship. One of the largest, the *William A. Irvin*, was the flagship of U.S. Steel's "Silver Stackers." The ship is 610 feet long, six stories tall, and could transport 14,000 tons of ore when fully loaded. When running empty back to Duluth for another load, the crew would play baseball in its empty holds.

The *Irvin* cruised the lakes from 1938 to 1986, when it was retired to the docks and made a floating maritime museum. Today's tours include visits to the ship's elaborate staterooms once used by industry bigwigs. Be sure to hoot and holler when you get to the massive, empty holds— the guides don't mind and the echo is amazing. If you come in October, local teenagers will have turned the *Irvin* into the *Ship of Ghouls*.

SS William A. Irvin, 350 Harbor Dr., Duluth, MN 55802

(218) 722-7876 or (218) 722-5573

Hours: June–August, Sunday–Thursday 9 A.M.–6 P.M., Friday–Saturday 9 A.M.–8 P.M.;
 September–May, call ahead

Cost: Adults $6.75, Seniors (65+) $5.75, Kids (3–12) $4.50

www.williamairvin.com

Directions: Railroad St. south from Lake Ave. (just east of I-35), then left on Harbor Dr.

GOOD-BYE, *EDMUND FITZGERALD*

Well, if you listen to Gordon Lightfoot, you know that Great Lakes shipping isn't all fun and games. The 729-foot-long SS *Edmund Fitzgerald* snapped in half during a storm on November 10, 1975, near the Soo Locks off Michigan's Upper Peninsula. The doomed ship took 29 unlucky crew members down with it. The *Edmund Fitzgerald* originated in Duluth on November 9 at the Burlington Northern Terminal. It headed north, past Silver Bay's Split Rock Lighthouse (Route 61, (218) 226-6377, www.mnhs.org), which remembers the freighter each year on November 10 by illuminating its beacon.

Despite its depressing ending, the song did generate nostalgia for the industry. Duluth, the largest freshwater port in the world, does everything it can to capitalize on that sentiment. Check out the *Duluth Shipping News* (www.duluthshippingnews.com) or the Boatwatcher's Hotline, (218) 722-6489, to find out when the big ones are coming into port, or heading back out. When they do, you'll be able to see the world's largest aerial lift bridge in action.

DULUTH

Duluth has earned many strange nicknames:

★ The Air-Conditioned City

★ The Center of the Universe

★ The Hay Fever Relief Haven of America

★ The San Francisco of the North

★ The Old Maid City, Looking Under Her Bed Every Night for an Ocean

---

The Minnesota state bird.

Effie
World's Largest Mosquito

Minnesotans like to joke that the mosquito, not the loon, should be the state bird. If that's the case, the bloodsucker behind Effie's town sign should be the state pterodactyl—it's a full six feet long, and it looks thirsty!

Don't worry that it's some sort of mutation that just flew out of the Chippewa National Forest—it's only a statue. Why anyone would want to honor the insect that makes summers up here so unpleasant is anyone's guess. Unless, perhaps, the locals are trying to scare away land developers.

Routes 1 & 38, Effie, MN 56639

No phone

Hours: Always visible

Cost: Free

Directions: On the southwest corner of the town's only intersection.

A lot of cursing went into these fenceposts.

Ely
Root Beer Lady Memorial

Dorothy Molter's story is as quaint and syrupy as a bottle of homemade root beer—what a coincidence that it is *about* homemade root beer. Molter was a registered nurse from Chicago who fell in love with the Boundary Waters in 1934. She moved into a cabin on Knife Lake and never left. Over time she developed quite a following of visitors who were willing to row their canoes almost to the Canadian border for a bottle of her famous root beer, a brew "that made Milwaukee jealous." How sweet.

But there's another side of the story, one in which this feisty little old lady sticks her finger in the eye of the federal government. When the Department of the Interior asked her to vacate her cabin in 1975, she mobilized her more than 6,000 yearly visitors to write letters demanding that an exception be made in her case. She eventually won, and lived for another 11 years, brewing 12,000 bottles a season using water scooped from the lake. Yummy.

After her death in 1986 at the age of 79, her legion of fans transported her cabin to the town of Ely where today it serves as a museum. You can now thumb through her guestbooks, check out the fence she made from broken paddles, or sip a bottle of root beer brewed using her original recipe—but hopefully made with tap water.

Dorothy Molter Memorial Foundation, 2002 E. Sheridan St., Ely, MN 55731
(218) 365-4451
Hours: May, Saturday–Sunday 10 A.M.–6 P.M.; June–August, daily 10 A.M.–6 P.M.
Cost: Adults $4, Kids (6–16) $2
www.canoecountry.com/dorothy
Directions: Two blocks east of the Rte. 1 intersection on Rte. 169 (Sheridan St.).

EVELETH
The nation's first polka mass was celebrated at Resurrection Catholic Church (301 Adams Avenue) in Eveleth on May 5, 1973.

ELY
"The two worst places I've ever heard of are Ely and Hell, the difference being there is a railroad out of Ely." —Billy Sunday

---

After Ely booster Leonard Zupancich passed away, his friends mixed his ashes with a rocket to be used for the town's Fourth of July celebration. His ashes were then blown all over the town.

Mother of all pucks.

Eveleth
United States Hockey Hall of Fame

As hard as it might be to believe, the often violent game of hockey has its roots in a dainty sport called ice polo where a rubber ball was used instead of a hard puck. That's one of the hundreds of interesting hockey facts you'll learn at this mega-museum to the sport of the scarred and toothless. The Hockey Hall of Fame opened in 1973 to cover all aspects of the sport, from the science of skate development to the personal tastes of hockey lovers. If you like history, you can admire the fourth Zamboni ever built, a 1956 model still in working condition. Are you a movie lover? Check out the gigantic fake scoreboard from Disney's *The Mighty Ducks*. Or peruse the museum's long list of famous players. Every inductee to the U.S. Hockey Hall of Fame has a pylon emblazoned with his name and accomplishments on it, along with a lockerful of the player's memorabilia. Did you know Gordie Howe had his own version of Honey Nut Toasted Oats and Frosted Flakes? You do now!

If the museum leaves you wanting more, head down the street to the World's Largest Hockey Stick and the World's Largest Puck (Grant Avenue and Monroe Street). The original three-ton stick was made in 1995 by Christian Brothers of Warrod, Minnesota. It contained enough white and yellow aspen to make 3,000 standard-issue sticks. Sadly, the elements took their toll, and the 107-foot-long sculpture rotted away.

But don't fret! A new stick has been ordered, and pieces of the first one can be purchased around town for a mere $5 donation. As with its predecessor, the new Bunyan-sized stick will be poised to slap a 700-pound, 5-foot puck. That's enough to knock out the goalie's back teeth!

801 Hat Trick Ave., PO Box 657, Eveleth, MN 55734

(800) 443-7825 or (218) 744-5167

Hours: January–April, Tuesday–Saturday 9 A.M.–5 P.M., Sunday 11 A.M.–3 P.M.;
   May–December, Monday–Saturday 9 A.M.–5 P.M., Sunday 11 A.M.–3 P.M.

Cost: Adults $3.50, Seniors (60+) $3, Teens (13–17) $3, Kids (6–12) $2.75

www.ushockeyhall.com

Directions: Museum just off Rte. 53 at Industrial Park Rd.; Puck and Stick downtown
   at the intersection of Grant and Monroe Sts., one block north of Rte. 7.

FLOODWOOD
On November 12, 1968, Uno Keikkile spotted a Bigfoot jumping out of a tree 10 miles north of Floodwood.

GARRISON
A 15-foot fiberglass Robin Hood guards the entrance to the Sherwood Forest RV Park (21927 Route 169) northeast of Garrison.

GRAND RAPIDS
Grand Rapids remembers "Mosquito Day" each year with a celebration of the "state bird" at the Forest History Center (2609 County Road 76).

Garrison
Aksarben Gardens

Hugo and Arnold Vogt had no time for women—they had plenty of projects to keep them busy. The biggest project had to be Aksarben Gardens on Bay Lake. (*Aksarben* is *Nebraska* spelled backward; the brothers spent their winters in Omaha.) Starting in 1918, the brothers built their "Eveless Paradise" out of rocks, cement, and a lot of sweat. Hugo constructed the towers, bridges, wishing wells, and waterfall that fed a moat. Arnold planted every square inch of free space with elaborate gardens.

During the 1930s, Aksarben Gardens was a popular roadside attraction. Sightseers paid 25¢ a head to take the tour, usually led by one of the barefoot Vogts in bib overalls. Clark Gable, Norma Talmadge, and Will Rogers were among the visitors. The highlight of the tour came when a bell on the dock summoned fish to the shore to be fed, earning Bay Lake the nickname "Tame Fish Lake."

After the brothers' deaths, the six-acre spread was carved up into smaller plots. Most of the structures remain but are not open to visitors. However, they can be seen from an adjoining road.

27527 Tame Fish Lake Rd., Garrison, MN 56450

No phone

Hours: Daylight hours; view from road

Cost: Free

Directions: Northwest of town, on Rte. 14 (Tame Fish Lake Rd.), east of Rte. 6.

Grand Rapids
There's No Place Like Home!

Frances Ethel Gumm was born in this small Minnesota town on June 10, 1922. Never heard of her? Perhaps you know her better by her stage name: Judy Garland! Of course, that wasn't her first stage name. She debuted as Baby Gumm at the ripe old age of two, singing "Jingle Bells" at her father's New Grand Theater on Pokagama Avenue. When the future Ms. Garland was four, her family pulled up stakes and headed for California. The old story was that her father knew he had talented daughters and was looking for bigger stages than could be found in northeast Minnesota, but the real reason was that he had been discovered to be having an affair with a young man in town and was leaving to avoid the scandal. Perhaps it was the age at which she left, or the manner in which the family departed, or the prescription drug abuse later in life, but Garland often told people she was from Grand Rapids, *Michigan*.

When you come to Grand Rapids, there are three main fan stops. The first is Garland's birthplace, restored in 1996, on the south side of town. The Gumm sisters would practice on the first-floor landing while their parents plinked out tunes on the piano. Behind the home is an Oz-themed garden filled with red poppies that may or may not put you to sleep. (The Gumm Family also lived at 727 Second Avenue NE, but that privately owned home is not open to the public.)

Judy Garland Birthplace & Museum, 2727 Route 169, PO Box 724, Grand Rapids, MN 55744

(800) 664-JUDY or (218) 327-9276 or (218) 326-1900

E-mail: jgarland@uslink.net

Hours: May–October, daily 10 A.M.–5 P.M.; November–April by appointment

Cost: Adults $3, Kids $3

www.judygarlandmuseum.com

Directions: South of town 1.5 miles on Rte. 169.

For still more Judy- and Oz-abilia, visit the Children's Museum run by the same organization that runs the birthplace. They've got one of the green coats from the Emerald City, a Winkie sword from the Wicked Witch of the West's Castle, and the carriage in which Dorothy and company rode through the Emerald City, pulled by a horse of a different color. The big crowd pleaser is the blue gingham dress Garland wore for a *Wizard of Oz* screen test.

Children's Discovery Museum, 19 Fourth St. NE, Grand Rapids, MN 55744

(866) CDM-KIDS or (218) 326-1900

Hours: Monday–Saturday 10 A.M.–5 P.M., Sunday Noon–5 P.M.

Cost: Adults $3, Kids $3 ($1 discount if ticket to birthplace purchased and used on the same day)

www.cdmkids.org

Directions: Downtown, on Rte. 2 (Fourth St.).

Final stop: the old Central School. Judy wasn't old enough to attend classes here, but she might have if the family had stayed in town. When the school was converted to a museum and restaurant, boosters sold yellow bricks for $55 each to pave the walkways out front (several were purchased by or dedicated to surviving Munchkins). The sale raised a million dollars, part of which they spent on exact replicas of the ruby slippers from *The Wizard of Oz*. They've also got artifacts from the Gumm family.

Itasca County Historical Museum, Old Central School, 10 Fifth St. NW, Grand Rapids, MN 55744

(800) GRAND-MN or (218) 326-6431

Hours: June–August, Monday–Saturday 9:30 A.M.–5 P.M., Sunday 10 A.M.–4 P.M.; September–May, Monday–Saturday 9:30 A.M.–5 P.M.

Cost: Adults $4, Seniors (55+) $3, Kids (6–12) $2

www.grandmn.com

Directions: One block north of the intersection of Rtes. 2 (Fourth St.) and 169 (Pokagama Ave.).

Grand Rapids celebrates the Judy Garland Festival each June. If you plan to visit, don't put it off. The Munchkins are dropping fast, and you won't be seeing them after the last of their kind have passed over the rainbow.

Information: (800) 664-JUDY

GRAND MARAIS

The Kadunce River northeast of Grand Marais was once known as the Diarrhea River. Drinking its water was not a good idea.

HIBBING

Baseballer **Roger Maris** was born in Hibbing on September 10, 1934.

HILL CITY

It is against the law for cats to chase dogs up trees or telephone poles in International Falls.

A 9-foot fiberglass bear stands along Route 169 in Hill City.

Hibbing
Bob Dylan's Boyhood Home

Robert Allen Zimmerman, better known as Bob Dylan, was born in Duluth on May 24, 1941, though he never considered that town his home. (The family's former house in Duluth (519 N. 3rd Avenue E) was sold to a fan on eBay in June 2001 for $94,600.) When the future music sensation was six, the Zimmermans moved to Hibbing, a town populated by the families of miners and loggers.

Truth be known, Dylan barely thought of Hibbing as his hometown either. He described it in "North Country Blues" as ". . . cardboard filled windows/And old men on the benches/Tell you now that the whole town is empty. . . The stores one by one they're a-foldin.'" He graduated from Hibbing High School (800 E. 21st Street) in 1959, and his yearbook listed his ambition as "To join Little Richard." Unlike everyone else's ambitions, his actually came true.

For a long time Hibbing felt rightly slighted by Mr. Bigshot Rock Star. Dylan returned here for a few days in 1968 when his father died. (The closest place he's ever performed has been Duluth . . . in 1998.) But the town is coming around . . . slowly. The library (2020 E. 5th Avenue, 10 A.M.–9 P.M.) has a small display dedicated to Dylan, but it's in the basement and few know it's there. There's no memorial plaque yet at the Androy Hotel (2010 5th Avenue E) where he was bar mitzvahed. And there's no mention of the significance of the home on 7th Avenue, either.

Give it time, babe.

Boyhood Home, 2425 Seventh Ave. E, Hibbing, MN 55746

Private phone

Hours: Private residence; view from street

Cost: Free

www.geocities.com/SoHo/Studios/7855/4hibbingmain.html

Directions: At the corner of 7th Ave. E and 25th St.

ISLAND LAKE

Bigfoot was spotted running across somebody's yard in Island Lake near Duluth on January 26, 1973.

Greyhound as a Pup

When Carl Wickman and Andrew Anderson set out to found the world's first bus service in 1914, they faced one major hurdle: nobody had invented the bus. Wickman was a disgruntled ex-miner who had sunk all his savings into a one-car Hupmobile dealership, but no one wanted to buy his only model. While waiting for that first sale, he ferried miners back and forth to the Hull-Rust Mine at 15¢ a head.

The taxi service turned out to be more lucrative than the dealership, so much so that Wickman asked Anderson's help to "stretch" the Hupmobile to add more seats. With the help of businessman Charles Wenberg, the Mesaba Transportation Company was born, as was the world's first bus.

When it later moved its base of operations to Chicago, the Mesaba Transportation Company became Greyhound. You'll get the whole story at the new Greyhound Museum. They've got a wide variety of the buses, from the first Hupmobile to a double-decker model. You can also trace the evolution of the company uniform, hear tapes of drivers' stories, and see toys and knickknacks licensed by the company. You'll also see the world's first bookmobile once used by the Hibbing library to bring books to mining camps.

Greyhound Museum, 1201 E. Greyhound Blvd. (3rd Ave.), Hibbing, MN 55746

(218) 263-6485 or (218) 262-3895 or (218) 263-5814

Hours: May–September, Monday–Saturday, 9 A.M.–5 P.M., Sunday 1–5 P.M.

Cost: Adults $3, Students $2, Kids (6–12) $1

www.greyhoundbusmuseum.org

Directions: Just north of the North Hibbing Cemetery, just past 13th St. N.

KINNY

Kinny seceded from the union on July 13, 1977, because it could not get a federal water project. Instead, it decided to apply for foreign aid.

LITTLE FALLS

On August 1, 1957, tin foil and tinsel dropped from the skies over Little Falls.

This is why you should recycle.

Hell of a Hole

When you're in Hibbing, you're in the heart of the Mesabi Iron Range. Oddly, the region's largest geographic feature isn't a mountain that goes up, but a pit that goes down: the Hull-Rust Mahoning Mine. This hole holds the record for the world's largest open-pit mine, and whoa doggie, is it big: 3 miles long, 2 miles wide, and 535 feet deep. In fact, it can be seen from outer space!

The mine is just north of Hibbing, or, more accurately, the town is just south of the mine. Hibbing used to be where the mine is today, but had to be moved when the open-pit got too large and threatened to swallow the town. The whole place was dragged to its new location beginning around 1920, earning it the nickname the Town That Moved Overnight. (Not true—it took about five decades.) You can still see the remnants of the street signs on your way to the Hull-Rust Mahoning overlook.

401 Penobscot Rd., Hibbing, MN 55746

(218) 262-4166

Hours: Always visible

Cost: Free; Guides on-site May–September, Monday–Saturday 9 A.M.–5 P.M., Sunday 1–5 P.M.

www.irontrail.org/Attractions/mining/Hull+Rust+Mahoning+Mine+View

Directions: North of town, on 3rd Ave., follow the signs.

STILL NOT SATISFIED?

If Hibbing's big hole hasn't convinced you that recycling is a good idea, here are a few more convincing stops in the general vicinity:

★ Virginia's **Mineview in the Sky** (Route 53, (800) 777-7395) offers a great view of the now-abandoned Rochleau open-pit mine from atop its Sky Lookout Tower. Millions of tons of taconite iron ore were yanked from this three-mile-long hole, carted away by vehicles like the King of the Lode, which is on display here. This dump truck is 44 feet long, 150 tons (unloaded), and its tires cost $29,000 . . . *each.*

★ The **Leonidas Overlook**, one mile west of Eveleth on Route 101, lets you survey the Eveleth Taconite Operations and the Minntac Mine. The overlook claims to be the highest human-made point on the Mesabi Iron Range (which seems to be getting lower by the minute.)

★ You can also view the Minntac Mine from the **Wacootah Overlook** south of Mountain Iron on Route 102.

★ Want to go to the bottom of one of these holes? Take a bus tour of the **Hill Annex Mine** near Calumet (www.dnr.state.mn.us/state_parks/hill/annex/mine/index.html, (800) 766-6000 or (218) 247-7215), where digging ceased in 1978.

★ And if you're tired of *iron* mines, visit the **Croft Mine Historical Park** north of Crosby (Second Avenue E and Spalj Drive, (218) 546-5625), where copper was extracted. Guides will tell you about one 1,884-pound ore-rich rock that yielded 310,000 pennies.

Hinckley
The Hinckley Fire

Hinckley once bragged that it was the Town Built of Wood, which was a rather cocky title in the years immediately following the Great Chicago Fire and the disaster at Peshtigo, Wisconsin. By 1894, civic boosters could claim a new title: the Town Reduced to Ashes.

On September 1, a massive forest fire fueled by the discarded waste from unbridled local logging swept toward the town from the south consuming everything in its path. The wall of flames was said to be more than four miles high and was spotted as far away as Mason City, Iowa.

Seeing the fire headed their way, some residents sought refuge in a local gravel pit filled with stagnant water. Most of them survived. Others escaped on the Duluth Limited, Train Number 4. Engineer Jim Root drove the burning train to Skunk Lake, six miles north of town, and saved dozens of frantic riders. (Root died at the end of the line, his burned hand fused to the engine's throttle.) More folk escaped on the Eastern Minnesota line that left from a station on the east side of town. In all, 418 people perished in the 160,000-acre conflagration that swallowed up 12 communities in just four hours. The remains of 248 unidentified victims were buried in a mass grave.

Hinckley is proud of the heroism of its citizens during the inferno, and monuments to the dead are scattered around town. The gravel pit (2nd Street SE & Power Avenue S) is still there, as is Skunk Lake (Route 61), and both are well marked for ghoulish tourists like you. A granite obelisk honoring the victims stands on the east side of town (Route 48 west of I-35). But no visit would be complete without a stop at the Hinckley Fire Museum housed in the old western depot, erected in the ashes just after the smoke cleared. They've got charred artifacts such as the tinderbox from Root's train, a doll carried by a lucky child survivor, and plates fused together by the 1500°F flames. In another room you'll find a mannequin of station agent Thomas Dunn plunking out warnings on his telegraph. His last message was "I think I've stayed too long," and he was right. An enormous mural in red and orange by Cliff Letty re-creates the town's carnage in gruesome detail.

Hinckley Fire Museum, 106 Old Highway 61, PO Box 40, Hinckley, MN 55037
(320) 384-7338

Hours: May–October, Tuesday–Saturday 10 A.M.–5 P.M.

Cost: Adults $3, Seniors (62+) $2, Kids (6–12) 50¢

www.hinckleyfire.com

Directions: Two blocks north of Rte. 23 where it turns south, toward Mora.

International Falls
Big Thermometer

International Falls proudly proclaims itself to be the Icebox of the Nation, a sobriquet confirmed by the town's cartoon counterpart on *Rocky and Bullwinkle*: Frostbite Falls. Rather than try to mask its polar predicament, the town promotes it with Ice Box Days each January. If you're crazy enough to attend, you can participate in the Freeze Your Gizzard Blizzard Run or the Cold Pizza Delivery Race. Better still, hop through the hole chipped in a local lake for the Polar Bear Dip.

As a means to document the city's wicked weather, the town erected a 22-foot thermometer near the Smokey Bear Statue. (There's a larger thermometer in California's Mojave Desert, but that makes sense, because the temperature is higher there.) Why such a large thermometer in International Falls? Probably so that folks can still read the low temperature when the snow drifts are too high.

3rd St. & 6th Ave., International Falls, MN 56649

(800) FALLS-MN

Hours: Always visible

Cost: Free

www.rainylake.org

Directions: At the corner of 3rd St. and 6th Ave.

MINNESOTA WINTERS

Let the giant thermometer be a warning to you all—Minnesota winters can be deadly. Any winter in this part of the country can be harsh, but check out these big-ass blizzards:

1888 Between 100 and 150 died, mostly kids heading home from school, when a snowstorm hit western Minnesota on January 12.

1940 The Armistice Day Blizzard (November 11) killed 49 when the temperature dropped 60 degrees overnight.

1975 A January 10 blizzard killed 35, most buried under two feet of snow and drifts up to 20 feet deep.

Nag, nag, nag.

Smokey Bear Statue

The original Smokey Bear was found in New Mexico after a 1950 fire in the Lincoln National Forest. But Smokey Bear the *icon* was created by the National Park Service to remind campers of the danger of forest fires. And while the real Smokey Bear is buried in his home state, the icon bear is memorialized in International Falls. (Incidentally, you read correctly—officially speaking, he's Smokey Bear, not Smokey *the* Bear.)

The 26-foot fiberglass statue was built in 1953 by Gordon Schumaker. Smokey appears to be a single dad, for two young cubs cling to his knees. "Prevent Forest Fires" is painted on the statue's base, a message all the more important in International Falls where the town's main industry is paper milling.

Smokey Bear Park, 3rd St. & 6th Ave., International Falls, MN 56649

(800) FALLS-MN

Hours: Always visible

Cost: Free

Directions: At the corner of 3rd St. and 6th Ave.

Kettle River
Not Her Again . . .

There was a time when the Virgin Mary was happy to have a manger to sleep in, but according to Stephen Marino, those days are over. Starting in 1991, the Mother of God started talking to this Green Bay, Wisconsin, resident and asking that he build her a 10,000-seat chapel and a seven-story housing complex. What's more, she didn't want it built in Green Bay (Vikings fans, take note) but in the tiny community of Kettle River, Minnesota.

To help him in his task, Mary claimed she would appear on the 15-acre plot of land Marino purchased north of town—on Easter Sunday, no less! The Duluth diocese denounced Marino (and partner Earl Nett) as hucksters. No doubt they were concerned that the event would cut into local churches' collection plates on the biggest revenue-generating day of the year.

Still, thousands flocked to the 193-person town to see the miracle, which was scheduled to go down at 3 P.M. Lots of visitors claimed to see the sun spinning, but nobody saw the Mother of God. The no-show put a dent in the fundraising efforts and, to date, nobody has broken the holy ground.

"Field of the Cross," Rte. 73, Kettle River, MN 55757

Hours: Always visible; view from road

Cost: Free

Directions: Four miles north of town, just west of Rte. 73 at the intersection with Rte. 14.

Lindstrom
Coffee Pot Tower

Is this just the latest step in Starbuck's quest for world domination, substituting a coffee pot for the town's water tower? Have no fear, this gigantic Swedish-style pot might look like a percolator, but it used to hold water . . . or at least it did so from 1902 to 1990. "Välkommen till

Lindström," a sign on the pot proclaims with the manic enthusiasm of an overcaffeinated Stockholmian.

Lindstrom is proud of its Swedish heritage, and apparently Swedes must drink a lot of coffee. The tower is illuminated at night, and under special atmospheric conditions will belch condensed steam out of its spout.

First Ave. N, Lindstrom, MN 55045

Hours: Always visible

Cost: Free

www.lindstrom.mn.org/gallery/views.htm

Directions: One block north of Lake Ave. (Rte. 8) in the center of town.

Little Falls
Charles A. Lindbergh House and History Center

Though he was born in Detroit in 1902, aviator Charles Lindbergh grew up in Washington, D.C., and in this small farmhouse in Little Falls. His father was a congressman on the Progressive ticket, and was best known (and criticized) for speaking out against U.S. involvement in World War I. Young Charles would spend his summers here where he combated boredom by inventing devices to haul ice into the house, hatched chickens in the dining room, and built hiding places into the walls for his valuables. One of his less successful inventions was a device used to keep animal organs alive outside their dead owners—Lucky Lindy was a Frankenstein wannabe!

You'll learn all this and more on your tour of the old Lindbergh home. Though it is filled with family keepsakes, the structure itself had to be restored after souvenir hunters walked off with many pieces of the building. One item nobody ever took was Moo Pond, a concrete duck bath Lindbergh made in 1919. Adjacent to the home is a museum with pieces of *The Spirit of St. Louis* and his first airplane, a Curtiss Jenny.

1620 S. Lindbergh Dr., Little Falls, MN 56345

(320) 632-3154

E-mail: lindbergh@mnhs.org

Hours: May–August, Monday–Saturday 10 A.M.–5 P.M., Sunday Noon–5 P.M.; September–October, Saturday 10 A.M.–4 P.M., Sunday Noon–4 P.M.

Cost: Adults $5, Seniors $4, Kids (6–12) $3

www.mnhs.org/places/sites/lh/index.html

Directions: Two miles south of town along the Great River Road (Rte. 52).

Mora
World's Largest Dala Horse

Those of you who aren't Swedish probably don't know the significance of the Dala horse legend, which in 1716 was said to play an important role in the survival of the Swedish state. Soldiers fighting under King Charles XII were forced to seek quarters in the homes of Swedish citizens in the province of Dalarna. To curry favor with their hosts, they carved wooden horses for children to play with. Most were painted orange, the easiest color paint to find. The little equines soon became the national toy.

In actuality, they probably were just something 18th-century loggers whittled to pass the time in the evenings—but isn't the legend a better story?

Mora, Sweden, is in the center of the Dalarna province and is the focal point of this folk craft. Mora, Minnesota, is the town's sister city. In a Texas-like gesture, the Mora Jaycees erected this ton-and-a-half, 22-foot-tall fiberglass Dala horse in 1971 at the town's fairgrounds.

Kanabec County Fairgrounds, Union St. S, Mora, MN 55051

(800) 291-5792

Hours: Always visible

Cost: Free

Directions: Two blocks north of the Rte. 65/23 split on Union St., at Ford Ave.

Ranier and Barnum
Big Vic, the Protest Colossus, and Big Louie, the Clone

Vic Davis didn't like getting pushed around. If you pushed him, he was going to push back. So when the U.S. Park Service wanted to take away his Cranberry Island in the late 1970s to make it part of Voyageurs National Park, he came up with a two-part plan. First, he sold off small plots to his friends at $19.95 a square foot, thereby complicating the feds' legal efforts to confiscate the land. Then, to show the Park Service he meant business, he ordered a 25-foot replica of himself (dressed in voyageur garb and leaning on a mighty big musket) and had it mounted on his island, smack dab in the middle of Rainy Lake. He dubbed the statue Big Vic, the Protest Colossus.

The rangers were not pleased with the park's new, 2,300-pound, fiber-glass attraction; nor did they appreciate the picnic area Davis had installed for visitors. They fined the helicopter pilot who delivered it for violating

Canadian airspace on the trip near the border. They eventually mounted an amphibious landing on Cranberry Island, kicked Davis off his property, and confiscated Big Vic.

The Park Service wouldn't return Big Vic unless Davis would agree not to re-erect it. Instead, they paid him a fraction of what the statue was worth and considered the issue settled. But Davis just took the money and ordered another from the same Wisconsin firm that had manufactured the first. In 1982 he mounted Big Louie, the Clone, next to the Voyageurs National Park Visitors Center, glaring down at those who'd kidnapped his brother. (Or was Big Vic his *father*?)

The government threatened to seize Big Louie, too. Davis had already made his point by generating a tornado of media coverage, so he took Big Louie down. The U.S. District Court ordered the government to pay Davis $90,000 for the island, and the case was finished.

Sort of. The Park Service didn't want Big Vic—they'd *never* wanted him—so they donated the statue to the town of Ranier. Today, the voluminous voyageur guards the entrance to the town, and the national park.

Big Vic, Rtes. 332 & 11, Ranier, MN 56668
No phone
Hours: Always visible
Cost: Free
Directions: Three miles east of International Falls on Rte. 11.
And what happened to Big Louie? Davis didn't want him any more than the Park Service did, so he sold the statue to a restaurant in Barnum.
Big Louie, Wyndtree North Restaurant, 3696 Main St. E, Barnum, MN 55707
No phone
Hours: Always visible
Cost: Free
Directions: Just west of I-35 at the Rte. 6 (Main St.) Exit.

ST. CLOUD
Starfish fell from the sky over St. Cloud on April 21, 1985. The species originated in Florida.

Put on some pants.

BIG VOYAGEUR COUNTRY

Big Vic and Big Louie aren't the only voyageur statues in this neck of the woods. Today there are literally dozens of wooden voyageurs carved with chainsaws out of dead trees on the courthouse squares of North Woods towns. But they all shrink when compared to four very large voyageurs erected in the northeastern part of the state.

BIG VOYAGEUR COUNTRY

The first, the Crane Lake Voyageur, was built in 1958 by Robert Bertil Ed, and guards the U.S.–Canadian border near the end of the road in the Superior National Forest. It stands 13.5 feet tall, is made of fiberglass, and leans on an enormous paddle. A sign at its base points out that he is wearing the "gay garb of these courageous happy men." Crane Lake celebrates Voyageur Days each year, in his honor.

Rtes. 24 & 424, Crane Lake, MN 55725
(800) 362-7405
Hours: Always visible
Cost: Free
Directions: Follow Rte. 24 into Crane Lake.

Two years after the Crane Lake Voyageur went up, the folks in Two Harbors erected a large French trapper of their own. Pierre the Voyageur was designed by Stanley Nelson in 1960, and was ages ahead of his northern counterpart. Pierre was 20 feet tall, his eyes moved back and forth, and he talked! He also doesn't seem to be wearing any pants.

But the Minnesota winters have taken their toll on the statue's mechanisms. Sadly, Pierre isn't talking anymore nor does he wag his head. Yet he is far from ready to crumble, as he was fabricated out of concrete. Think of him as the strong, silent type.

Voyageur Motel, 1227 7th Ave., Two Harbors, MN 55616
(218) 834-3644
Hours: Always visible
Cost: Free
Directions: On Rte. 61 (7th Ave.) at 13th St.

Farther south, in Cloquet, a fiberglass voyageur was erected outside the town's Tourist Information Office in 1976. He carries the obligatory paddle and he's the same height as the Two Harbors trapper. But unlike the other statues, he actually has a face you can recognize. Is that Foster Brooks? Without the ability to talk or move, he pales by comparison to the Two Harbors trapper.

Rte. 33, Cloquet, MN 55720
No phone
Hours: Always visible
Cost: Free
Directions: North of Rte. 33 from I-35.

BIG VOYAGEUR COUNTRY CONTINUED

If size matters most to you, head even farther south to Pine City, site of a 35-foot wooden voyageur. The statue is not carved from a pine, as you might expect in Pine City, but from an old-growth California redwood, transported here in the 1970s. Some claim it is the World's Largest Chainsaw Sculpture. Yes, it might seem ironic, perhaps even idiotic, to mow down an ancient redwood to erect a monument to living in the great outdoors. If you have a complaint, bring it up with Paul Bunyan—he's the one who chopped it down.

Pine City was a natural choice for such a monument, even if the statue wasn't made of pine, for it was here that the North West Company established a fur trading post in 1804 along the Snake River. Today, the site has been restored by the Minnesota Historical Society and is open to tourists (Route 7 west of town, (320) 629-6356, www.mnghs.org/places/sites/nwcfp/index.html).

Riverside Park, 1st Ave. & Main St., Pine City, MN 55063
No phone
Hours: Always visible
Cost: Free
Directions: On the north end of town on 6th St. (Main St.), just north of the river.

St. Augusta
Ventura, By Any Other Name . . .

. . . would smell as sweaty. In what must have seemed like a good idea at the time, the small, unincorporated community of St. Augusta decided in May 2000 to change its name to Ventura in honor of the state's new governor. Well, it was actually more the town council's idea—the locals weren't thrilled with the switch. It was a shameless PR stunt intended to draw tourists, not unlike what the pro-wrestling governor might have pulled. Instead, it drew ridicule . . . from *everywhere.*

Voters petitioned to get a resolution placed on the November 2000 ballot to have the name changed back to St. Augusta. It passed by a wide margin. (Incidentally, there is no reason to believe the town won't change its name again; the town was also once called Berlin, and then Neenah.)

All Over Town, St. Augusta, MN 56301

No phone

Hours: Always visible

Cost: Free

Directions: On Rte. 7, south of I-94 at St. Cloud.

Sandstone
Tim Allen, Prisoner

Talk about a lucky guy! Twenty-five-year-old Timothy Allen Dick was busted on October 2, 1978, in the Kalamazoo, Michigan, airport parking lot for trafficking cocaine. He was snared in an undercover sting set up by the Michigan state police. Dick pleaded no contest, and was sentenced to between three and seven years in a federal facility in Sandstone.

He was understandably nervous about his pending incarceration, due in no small part to his last name. He decided to stick to himself and read a lot. He fended off trouble with his sense of humor. And it worked . . . big time. Twenty-eight months later he was released, changed his name to Tim Allen, and started working the stand-up comedy circuit. His everyman routine eventually became the basis for the TV series *Home Improvement*.

Sandstone Federal Correctional Institution, Kettle River Rd., PO Box 999,

 Sandstone, MN 55072

(320) 245-2262

Hours: Always visible

Cost: Free

www.pop.gov/facilnot.html

Directions: North of town.

SKIBO

Residents of Skibo spotted UFOs over nearby Hoyt Lake on October 10, 1990. Two police officers then saw several objects hovering over the water, and three to five objects were confirmed on Duluth radar.

How new cars are made. *Landing on Eros* **by Tamsie Ringler, 2001. 1987 Mercury Sable and 1988 Chevy Corsica (top).**

Shafer
Franconia Sculpture Park

Ah, art the way it's supposed to be: not locked up in a stuffy museum, but scattered around an open field where folks can enjoy it! The Franconia Sculpture Park is a fascinating, hilarious, evolving, educational conglomeration of works by artists in residence and workshop participants.

Currently there are more than 70 works in this 16-acre field, but there's plenty of room for more. Most of the pieces tend to be industrial—huge, metal structures made from recycled materials—but there is no guarantee as to what you'll find. Here are some titles: *UFO (Unidentified Found Objects). Troccoaster. A Certain Kind of Squirrel. Variability is the Enemy of Quality & Jolly-Wadi-Ma-Jig.*

Franconia Sculpture Park supports established and emerging artists, as well as school art groups. Unhampered by pressures from galleries, unpaid landlords, and confined spaces, resident artists are encouraged to innovate and explore their talents. The result is a mighty cool roadside attraction.

29815 Unity Ave., Shafer, MN 55074

(651) 465-3701

E-mail: info@franconia.org

Hours: Dawn to dusk

Cost: Free

www.franconia.org

Directions: On Rte. 8 between Shafer and Taylors Falls.

Silver Bay
Macaulay Culkin Near-Death Site

The best part of the dreadful movie *The Good Son* is seeing Macaulay Culkin dangle over a 200-foot rocky cliff, his life in the hands of his mother, who must choose between saving him or Elijah Wood. Sound like a simple decision? Well, she has to *think* about it . . . but just for a few seconds. The scene was filmed at Palisade Head, a rocky crag along the western shore of Lake Superior. You are kindly advised *not* to re-create the scene for your vacation photos.

Palisade Head, Tettegouche State Park, Route 61, Silver Bay, MN 55614

No phone

Hours: Daylight hours

Cost: Free

www.dnr.state.mn.us/state_parks/tettegouche/index.html

Directions: Two miles northeast of town on Rte. 61, watch for signs near the radio tower on the right side of the road.

SOUDAN
Soudan was named to poke fun at its freezing winters; founders thought it was the exact opposite of the Sudan in Africa.

Rocky is actually made of metal.

Rocky Taconite

The Village and Reserve Mining Company wanted to say "Thanks!" to taconite, the iron ore that made them rich. But how? It's rather difficult to talk to a rock. Instead, they invented a cartoonish character and dubbed him Rocky Taconite. This 12-foot, roly-poly miner was welded together from old storage tanks and outfitted with a silver helmet, orange boots and gloves, and a pick. He stands atop a giant slab of his namesake ore.

Rocky has since become the unofficial mascot of Silver Bay. In 1990, he was moved to his present location, halfway up the hill overlooking town, so that more folks could see him. All hail, Taconite!

Outer Dr., Silver Bay, MN 55614

No phone

Hours: Always visible

Cost: Free

www.silverbay.com

Directions: Head up the hill from Rte. 61 at the north end of town on Rte. 5 (Outer Dr.).

Soudan
Soudan Underground Mine State Park

If you're interested in going deep beneath the earth's surface but you find caves filled with stalactites and stalagmites too "natural," perhaps the tour of the decommissioned Soudan Mine would be more to your liking. Every cubic inch of this hole in the ground was excavated by a human being. An elevator lowers you 2,341 feet—almost a half-mile—down the main shaft, leaving you 689 feet below sea level. Bring a coat, because it's 50°F down there, all year round.

The 90-minute tour takes you to the mine's deepest point, the 27th Level. Put on your miner's helmet! You'll ride an ore train through the tunnels, see hard-rock drills, and worry about what you would do if the power went out. But don't fret; known as the Cadillac of Mines, the Soudan had an impressive safety record: only three miners were killed here in accidents before it was closed in 1963. No tourists have met a similar fate. And the possibility of flooding from one of the surrounding lakes? Relax . . . they've got pumps!

1379 Stuntz Bay Rd., Tower, MN 55790

(800) 766-6000 or (218) 753-2245

Hours: May–September, daily 10 A.M.–4 P.M.

Cost: Adults $7, Kids (5–12) $5

www.dnr.state.mn.us/state_parks/soudan_underground_mine/index.html

Directions: Northeast of town off Rte. 169, follow the signs.

A long way from Heritage, USA.

South International Falls
Birthplace of Tammy Faye

Tammy Faye fans, come one, come all, to the place where it all began! Right here, on March 7, 1942, Tamara Faye LaValley entered the world during a blinding snowstorm. Her mother Rachel named her after a Russian ballerina she had heard about on a radio program.

When Tammy Faye was three, her mother divorced her cheating father Carl and married widower Fred Grover a few years later. Combined, they had four boys and four girls, all crammed into a small home in South International Falls, kind of like a North Woods Brady Bunch. The outhouse they all used is long gone, but the home looks about the same as it did then. When Tammy Faye was a teenager, she got a room of her own in the attic, just as Greg Brady did in his later teen years.

1614 3rd Ave. E, South International Falls, MN 56679
Private phone
Hours: Always visible; view from street

Cost: Free

Tammy Faye Fan Club: www.tammyfaye.com

Directions: Five blocks east of Rte. 11 (2nd Ave. W).

Because of the divorce, the local Assemblies of God (1309 3rd Avenue E) congregation shunned Tammy Faye's mother. Feeling the treatment of her mother unfair, Tammy Faye attended the Mission Covenant (1631 1st Avenue E) with her Aunt Gin. It was here during a fire-and-brimstone sermon that she first accepted the Lord. According to *Telling It My Way*, she rolled around on the altar speaking in tongues until long after the rest of the congregation had left for home.

Tammy Faye's religious awakening was not the only life-changing conversion she experienced during her teen years. In one of the girl's bathrooms at International Falls Senior High (1515 11th Avenue), her friend Ada DeRaad introduced her to mascara and ruby red lipstick. At the time, Tammy Faye had an after-school job at Woolworth's, which had a cosmetics counter. It was there, sometime in the late 1950s, that she purchased her first tube of mascara and realized that looking good was not a sin. From that point on, she never looked back . . . or if she did it was through her gloppy eyelashes.

Ronnings (formerly Woolworths), 301 3rd St., International Falls, MN 56649

(218) 283-8877

Hours: Monday–Saturday 9 A.M.–7 P.M., Sunday 9 A.M.–4 P.M.

Cost: Free

Directions: Just west of the intersection of Rtes. 53 and 11 (3rd St.).

After graduating from high school (where her yearbook quote read "Good things come in small packages"), Tammy Faye headed to the big city of Minneapolis and North Central Bible College. She roomed with a student named Aloha, a spunky redhead she described as having "wondrous boobs," and took two bubble baths a day.

At North Central she met Jim Bakker, from Muskegon, Michigan. Jim took Tammy Faye to church on their first date, and on the way home he proposed and gave her a bracelet. They were married on April Fool's Day, 1967, in the basement of the Minneapolis Evangelistic Auditorium. Later they learned the college forbade students from tying the knot while still attending classes, and they were expelled.

North Central Bible College, 910 Eliot Ave., Minneapolis, MN 55404

(612) 343-4400

Hours: Always visible

Cost: Free

www.ncbc.edu

Directions: One block east of Chicago Ave. S on 9th St.

Two Harbors
Hooray for Sandpaper!

Little rough around the edges? Why not stop on by the 3M/Dwan Sandpaper Museum? You can't use the sandpaper on display, but you'll receive a free sample on your way out.

The 3M (Minnesota Mining and Manufacturing) Corporation, founded in Two Harbors in 1902, did not set out to invent sandpaper; it just sort of happened. Years ago the company purchased what it thought was a corundum mine, but which turned out to be anorthosite. Corundum is used to make grinding wheels, but anorthosite crumbles into little pieces. In 1920, the company used magnetized glue to affix this previously worthless anorthosite powder to a waterproof paper surface, and sandpaper was born!

Oh, but that's not all you'll learn at this fascinating industrial museum. 3M also invented pressure-sensitive masking tape in 1928, Scotch tape in 1930, and Post-It Notes years later. The museum is housed in the former home of 3M cofounder John Dwan and looks for all the world like a miniature Home Depot under glass.

3M/Dwan Sandpaper Museum, PO Box 313, 201 Waterfront Dr., Two Harbors, MN 55616

(888) 832-5606 or (218) 834-4898

Hours: May–October, daily 9:30 A.M.–5 P.M.

Cost: Adults $1.50

Directions: Tours start at the Lake County Historical Society.

TWIG
The town of Twig was named for its original post office, which some joker called "a small branch" of the U.S. Postal Service.

Lighthouse B&B

Most bed-and-breakfasts are usually low-impact, low-stress lodging alternatives, but not the Lighthouse B&B in Two Harbors. The flashing beacon on this 1891 structure still operates, though it is controlled by a computer in Duluth. That doesn't let you off the hook, however. Though you may be a paying guest and the light is on autopilot, there are still chores to do, such as raising the flags, logging events in the journal, feeding the birds, and keeping 1,000-foot ships from running up on the rocky shoreline. The Lake County Historical Society expects you to take your task seriously. And if one of those freighters should sink, remember, they've got your credit card number.

1 Lighthouse Point, PO Box 128, Two Harbors, MN 55616

(888) 832-5606 or (218) 834-4898

E-mail: lakehist@lakenet.com

Hours: Open year-round

Cost: $99–$125/night

www.lighthousebb.org

Directions: Poplar St. (6th St.) south from Rte. 61 to the waterfront, follow the road to your right.

TWO HARBORS

An eight-foot fiberglass rooster stands outside Weldon's Gift Shop in Two Harbors (1065 Highway 61).

VIRGINIA

Radical priest **Daniel Berrigan** was born in Virginia on May 9, 1921.

The town of Virginia burned to the ground twice, in 1893 and 1900.

VOYAGEURS NATIONAL PARK

Voyageurs National Park is the only national park without a road.

I want YOU to buy a car.

Virginia
Uncle Sam Statue

With all the Paul Bunyans around the state, it's kind of nice to see some evidence that Minnesota is part of a larger entity: the U. S. of A. Drivers on Route 53 need no better reminder than the gigantic Uncle Sam at a

Virginia car dealership. But get this: Uncle Sam doesn't sell just Chryslers and Chevys, but also Japanese Toyotas. Has Sam betrayed the American autoworker, or is economic isolationism a thing of the past?

Don't think about it too much—it's just a fiberglass advertising gimmick.

Iron Trail Motors, 1301 17th St. S, Virginia, MN 55792

(800) 662-5779 or (218) 741-2355

E-mail: itm@irontrail.com

Hours: Always visible

Cost: Free

Directions: On Rte. 53, just east of the bend near the Rte. 169 merge.

World's Largest Floating Loon

Rush Limbaugh at the beach? No, he doesn't even come close . . .

Virginia, Minnesota, has a 21-foot-long, 9-foot-tall loon, and it's been bobbing in the middle of Silver Lake since 1982—winters excepted, of course. It was designed by William "Bill" Martin and built with the assistance of Larry Gentelli. According to people who keep track of such things, it is the World's Largest Floating Fiberglass Animal. Others claim it's the World's Largest Decoy, but since it's illegal to hunt this bird, the claim seems inaccurate, to say nothing of inappropriate.

The floating monument honors Minnesota's state bird, the common loon (*Gavia immer*). Virginia throws an annual Land of the Loon Festival each June.

Silver Lake, 9th Ave. S, Virginia, MN 55792

(800) 777-8497

Hours: Spring–Fall, always visible

Cost: Free

www.virginiamn.com

Directions: In the middle of Silver Lake in the center of town, off Olcott Park.

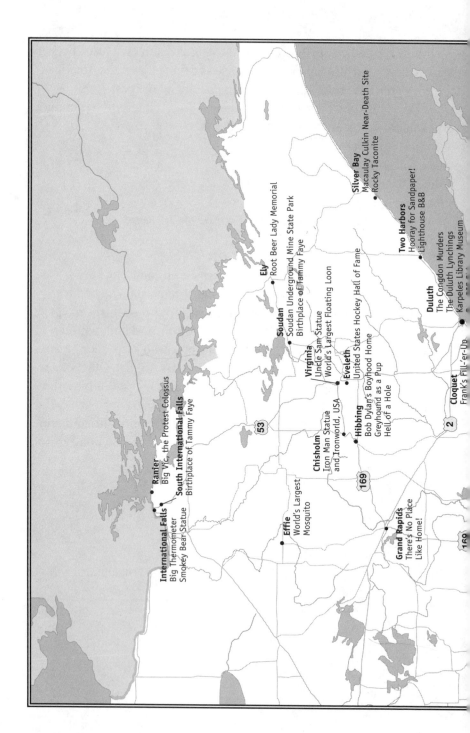

International Falls
Big Thermometer
Smokey Bear Statue

Ranier
Big Vic, the Protest Colossus

South International Falls
Birthplace of Tammy Faye

Effie
World's Largest
Mosquito

Chisholm
Iron Man Statue
and Ironworld, USA

Soudan
Soudan Underground Mine State Park
Birthplace of Tammy Faye

Ely
Root Beer Lady Memorial

Virginia
Uncle Sam Statue
World's Largest Floating Loon

Eveleth
United States Hockey Hall of Fame

Hibbing
Bob Dylan's Boyhood Home
Greyhound as a Pup
Hell of a Hole

Grand Rapids
There's No Place
Like Home!

Cloquet
Frank's Fill-'er-Up

Duluth
The Congdon Murders
The Duluth Lynchings
Karpeles Library Museum

Two Harbors
Hooray for Sandpaper!
Lighthouse B&B

Silver Bay
Macaulay Culkin Near-Death Site
Rocky Taconite

53

2

169

169

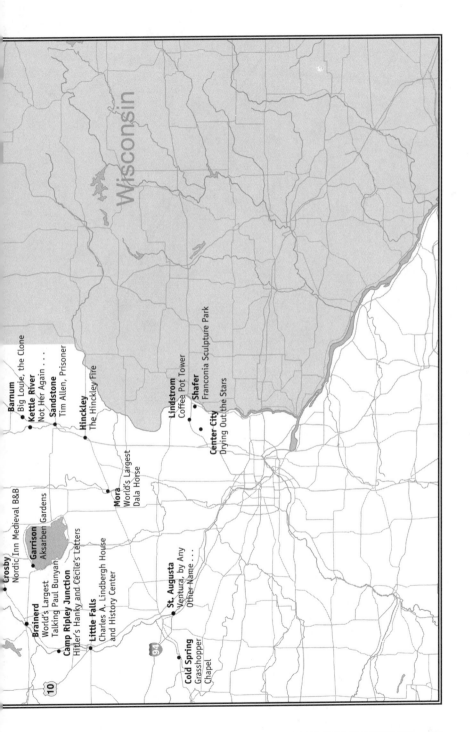

Wisconsin

Barnum
Big Louie, the Clone
Kettle River
Not Her Again . . .
Sandstone
Tim Allen, Prisoner

Hinckley
The Hinckley Fire

Lindstrom
Coffee Pot Tower
Shafer
Franconia Sculpture Park
Center City
Drying Out the Stars

Mora
World's Largest
Dala Horse

Crosby
Nordic Inn Medieval B&B
Garrison
Aksarben Gardens
Brainerd
World's Largest
Talking Paul Bunyan
Camp Ripley Junction
Hitler's Hanky and Cecile's Letters
Little Falls
Charles A. Lindbergh House
and History Center

St. Augusta
Ventura, by Any
Other Name . . .

Cold Spring
Grasshopper
Chapel

3

THE SOUTHWEST

Ask people to describe southwest Minnesota in one word, and "flat" is the word they often come up with. True enough, but it seems rather unfair to hold a featureless landscape against the local population, particularly when they're doing so much to dress the place up. Come to this corn-covered corner of the state and you'll find a gas station encrusted in beautiful geodes, a classic monument to a German warlord, the World's Largest Ball of Twine, and a town whose streets are named for the far reaches of our galaxy.

And are you looking for excitement? The region also boasts the Minnesota Inventors Hall of Fame! And the state's most daring water-ski team!! And a mummy once said to be the remains of Lincoln's assassin, John Wilkes Booth!!! And the World's Oldest Rock . . .

Well, you didn't think I could keep it up forever, did you?

Bring me your pebbles, your stones, your geodes, yearning to be cemented on my dress . . .

Arco
H. P. Pedersen Gas Station

The trouble with having a rock collection is that it's hard to get a non–rock lover to take the time to look at your fabulous finds. But, if you arrange your rocks in an aesthetically pleasing manner, you just may have a chance.

H. P. Pedersen had a pile of rocks on his farm when he bought the only gas station in Arco in 1936. Using cement, he encrusted the building's façade with elaborate rocky patterns, adding arches with suspended three-dimensional stars. When Pedersen died in 1942, his son Vernon expanded on the paterfamilias's vision by constructing a miniature village behind the station. And what Minnesota community would be complete without an oversized animal sculpture on the outskirts of town? Up went a gigantic Hugo the Ram, followed by other creations.

Vernon Pedersen eventually sold the station and moved away in 1952, but his family's legacy remains. Some of their pieces were taken by local relatives, but Hugo, a Statue of Liberty, and a Liberty Bell were moved to Anderson Community Park on Lake Stay. The rest of the village was given away or torn down. The filling station was converted into a private residence, but the front of the home looks very much the same as it did when Pedersen pumped gas there. That's because it's made of rocks . . . lots and lots of rocks.

Laurel & Hawthorn Sts., Arco, MN 56113

No phone

Hours: Always visible

Cost: Free

Directions: Gas station on Rte. 15 (Laurel St.); statues just east of town, north of Rte. 7, at Lake Stay.

CEYLON
Walter Mondale was born in Ceylon on January 5, 1928.

Ceylon was named for a box of Ceylon tea at a local general store.

DARFUR
According to local legend, the town of Darfur got its name when a local train came to a stop here and the Norwegian fireman asked the engineer, "Why you stop dar fur?"

They're not going to run out of milk any time soon.

Bongards
Big Cow

Nobody seems to know how this single fiberglass cow strayed so far from its Wisconsin herd, but it shows no apparent interest in returning. These big-ass bovines can be found all throughout the Cheese State, but in Minnesota? You'd think Packer-phobic Vikings fans would have hacked it up with their battle-axes by now.

Yet this 20-foot black-and-white Holstein has maintained her composure in hostile territory. Maybe she's been spared because she doesn't wear a foam cheesehead hat. Folks from the Bongards Creamery, a local co-op, like the attention she brings to their outlet store—so perhaps they're watching her back.

Bongards Creamery, 13200 Country Rd. 51, Bongards, MN 55322

(952) 466-5521

Hours: Always visible

Cost: Free

Directions: South on Rte. 51 from Rte. 212.

Cosmos
Spacey Town

Back in 1870, Daniel Hoyt had a farout idea for sleepy Nelsontown: he suggested the name of the village be changed to something more lofty and scientific. This done, perhaps a university could be convinced to relocate there. Locals were eventually coerced into renaming the town Cosmos.

But Hoyt didn't stop there. The town's east–west avenues were renamed after constellations (Orion, Draco, Vega, Libra, Pegasus, Capricorn, etc.), while the north–south streets were changed to planets (Venus, Mars, Jupiter, Saturn, etc.). Major roads were given special honors: Astro Boulevard (Route 7) and Milky Way (Route 4).

And did the universities, planetariums, and museums flock to Cosmos? Well, not exactly. But they do have a Silver Star Café.

All over town, Cosmos, MN 56228

No phone

Hours: Always visible

Cost: Free

Directions: At the intersection of Rtes. 4 and 7.

DELANO
A Simple Plan was filmed around Delano in 1998.

An 11-foot fiberglass chicken has been standing outside Flippin' Bill's Burgers & Chicken (County Line Road and Route 12) in Delano since 1990.

FAIRMONT
William Robert Livingston constructed a replica of the Lincoln Log Cabin in Fairmont (1300 N. North Avenue) in 1866, and, unlike the original cabin, it still stands.

Fairmount celebrates King Korn Days each September.

All wrapped up.

Darwin
World's Largest Ball of Twine (by a Single Person)

Some folks are content to spend their time on the sofa for hours on end watching professional wrestling or the Home Shopping Network. Not Francis Johnson. While everyone else was glued to the boob tube or canning pickles, he was out in his barn working on a project that would bring him a little fame, less fortune, and eventual death. Four hours a day, every day, Johnson wound scraps of twine onto an ever-expanding ball. Over the course of 29 years, from 1950 to 1979, he wrapped 17,400 pounds of twine around and around until it grew to a 12-foot diameter behemoth. By his calculations, if a gigantic kitten started batting that ball around, heading south, it would not be fully unwound until it reached the Gulf of Mexico.

The Guinness Book of World Records honored Johnson's accomplishment in 1979, but withdrew the title in 1994 when another ball of string surpassed Darwin's Minnesota miracle. As Johnson had been dead since 1989 (in part from emphysema aggravated by the chemicals used to treat the twine), he was unable to rise to the challenge of making his ball even larger.

The faithful citizens of Darwin have never acknowledged the Guinness demotion. They're quick to point out that of the two twine balls that are larger than theirs, one has been wrapped by a *team* in its Kansas community, and the other was made of lightweight *plastic* twine and was bankrolled by Ripley's Believe It or Not!, the very same organization that had tried unsuccessfully to buy out Johnson's ball after his death to move it to some museum in a tourist-trap town.

Darwin has moved the ball to a shed at the center of town, which is two blocks from the town's outskirts. On the second Saturday in August each year, Darwin celebrates Twine Ball Day. Weird Al Yankovic has written a song honoring Johnson called "The Biggest Ball of Twine in Minnesota," which volunteers at the town's Twine Ball Gift Shop will gladly sing for you. Be sure to stop by the Twine Ball Inn adjacent to the park; in it you'll find Johnson's collection of wooden pliers.

First & William Sts., Darwin, MN 55324

No phone

Hours: Always visible

Cost: Free

Directions: In a lot beneath the water tower, on Rte. 14 (First St.), south of Rte. 12.

FULDA
Fulda claims to be the Wood Duck Capital of the World.

GAYLORD
Gaylord calls itself the Egg Capital of the World and hosts an annual Eggstravaganza Festival.

GRANITE FALLS
Granite Falls celebrates Ole and Lena Days each February in honor of its Scandinavian heritage.

There's no place like Gnometown!

Dawson
Gnometown, USA

The children of Dawson have long been told the legend of how the gnomes came to their small Midwest town. Years ago, a meeting of the world's little people—leprechauns, pixies, faeries, sprites, and kobolds—decided to migrate to Minnesota, led by a gnome named Daws. They ended up in Dawson, where the local folk, to make things easier, lumped them all into one species: gnomes.

The whole ridiculous story has been etched on a kiosk in Dawson's Gnome Park. Scattered around the grassy field are dozens of concrete gnomes. Where did they come from? Every year since 1988, on the last weekend in June, the town celebrates Riverfest. During the festivities, one or more community leaders are honored with a personal gnome replica to be put on public display. Even if you're unfamiliar with the local population, the statues are easily recognized as doctors, teachers, and librarians. Most of the statues are located in an eastside park, but others can be found around town. The effect is a little unsettling; it's as if some gnome warlock has cast a spell on unfortunate citizens, turning them one by one into sacrificial statuary to an elfin god.

151 E. Oak St., Dawson, MN 56232

(320) 769-2981

Hours: Always visible

Cost: Free

www.dawsonmn.com

Directions: At the east end of town on Rte. 212 (Oak St.), between 1st and 2nd Sts.

Granite Falls
World's Oldest Rock

OK, so the thought of spending your vacation staring at a rock doesn't sound all that appealing—right? Well this isn't just any old rock, but *the* old rock; this museum's hunk of morton gneiss is more than 3.6 billion years old. Heck, the Earth is only 4.5 billion! While all the planet's early rocks were being ground up by tectonic action or slowly obliterated by erosion, this little stone was minding its own business. And now it's this museum's star attraction.

You're probably wondering who has the engrossing task of dating every rock on the planet. They're called geologists, and they love this sort of thing. Until one of them finds an older sample, this rock holds the record. And thanks to the efforts of the volunteers at the Yellow Medicine County Historical Museum, it probably will for some time to come—no continental plate moving at an inch a year is going to swallow up this building and its precious specimen on their watch!

Yellow Medicine County Historical Museum, 98 Highway 67 E, PO Box 145, Granite Falls, MN 56241

(320) 564-4479

E-mail: ymchs@kilowatt.net

Hours: Tuesday–Sunday 1–4 p.m.

Cost: Free

Directions: At the intersection of Rtes. 67 and 23.

Hanley Falls
Minnesota's Machinery Museum

Hanley Falls has some 200 residents, which, if you do the math, probably means that for every man, woman, and child in the community there exist 500 or so artifacts at the town's only museum. At its current rate of growth, the Minnesota Machinery Museum will someday take over the entire town.

The massive collection was started in the 1970s and housed in a WPA-era school at the center of Hanley Falls. The building wasn't modified much; classrooms were simply converted into themed exhibits. Horse stuff here. Quilting stuff there. Just open a door and start exploring. The overwhelming majority of the items—at least in terms of tonnage—are farm machinery, as the museum's name implies. Smaller machines are in the school gymnasium; the rest are scattered through four outbuildings.

Looking at all the rusty threshers and reapers and combines and planters and plows and tractors, it's no wonder so many farmers are missing fingers—this stuff looks dangerous! The museum also has a substantial collection of old autos. The local motto seems to be, "Don't throw it out, send it over to the museum. They'll find a place for it."

100 N. First St., Hanley Falls, MN 56245

(507) 768-3522 or (507) 768-3580

Hours: May–September, Wednesday–Monday 1–5 p.m.

Cost: Free; donations accepted

Directions: One block east of 3rd Ave. W on Main St.

Hendricks
This B&B Blows

If there's one natural resource that's readily available in this part of the Midwest, it's wind. With few trees, hills, or buildings to break gales from neighboring South Dakota, Hendricks is an ideal place to locate the Midwest Center for Wind Energy. To get a little more oomph from the gales, the center mounted its windmills atop the only bump around, the 200-foot-tall Buffalo Ridge. Gusts crest the hill, hit the massive turbine blades, and zing—electricity!!

The center's mission is primarily research-oriented, but it does have an educational component. And what better way to inform others about the benefits of this clean energy source than to have folks spend the night?

This unique B&B is set up with four singles and four doubles, and guests are encouraged to check out the work being done to break our nation's dependence on fossil fuels. While in some sense they're preaching to the converted—how many oil tycoons do you imagine would spend a night here?—there's still plenty to be learned during your stay.

Midwest Center for Wind Energy, RR 2, PO Box 203, Hendricks, MN 56136

(507) 275-4062

E-mail: bwilcox@windpower.com

Hours: Always open; call for reservations

Cost: $75–$100/night

www.windpower.com

Directions: You'll get directions when you make your reservation.

LITCHFIELD
By law, Litchfield couples can make out at drive-in movies, but only in the front seats of their cars.

MADISON
The town of Madison became the Lac Qui Parle county seat on November 12, 1886, when 150 residents and 40 horses dragged the courthouse from the town of Lac Qui Parle, 15 miles away, against that community's wishes.

MARSHALL
Marshall women may not shine their shoes on Saturday.

Alien mummy, or clever hoax?
Photo by author, courtesy of the McLeod County Historical Society

Hutchinson
The Mummy!

What is it??!? Five feet long, gray, and shriveled with long, black hair, it reclines in a glass-topped coffin, its mouth open in a final, silent scream. Hutchinson schoolchildren on field trips have been terrified for decades. Some say it's a Peruvian mummy, their story confirmed years ago by a South American exchange student. Older folk claim it's an Indian killed in a pioneer battle and preserved by a local undertaker with an Egyptian fetish. Others believe its oversized skull and E.T.-like eye sockets suggest an otherworldly origin; they also claim an x-ray of the mummy shows bronze pins in one of its upper legs. Interesting . . .

But museum curators tell a different story. Documents reveal that this unique specimen traveled the South for years as the mummified remains of John Wilkes Booth, or sometimes Jesse James, before ending up in this county's collection. For years the museum had it propped upright in a closet to scare visitors. Undignified? Perhaps. But you should at least know it's made out of papier-mâché. That's right—this Martian presidential assassin from Peru is a prop from some carney's attic, and now it's the museum's premier attraction.

Interestingly, the McLeod County Historical Society once had a more historic artifact in its collection, but they relinquished it in 1971. It was the skull of Little Crow, leader of the Sioux uprising. Though the conflict was over, Little Crow was gunned down near town while picking blueberries with his son.

McLeod County Historical Society, 380 School Rd. NW, Hutchinson, MN 55350

(320) 587-2109

Hours: Monday 10 A.M.–8 P.M., Thursday–Friday 10 A.M.–4 P.M., Saturday 1–4 P.M.

Cost: Adults $3, Seniors $2, Kids (6–18) $1

www.mcleodhistory.org

Directions: One block north of Rte. 7, four blocks east of the lake.

Luverne
Mystery Wall

Like the Egyptian Pyramids or Great Britain's Stonehenge, Luverne has its own piece of ancient architecture: the Mystery Wall. And though most of the questions regarding the previous structures have been explained, the 1,250-foot wall in Blue Mounds State Park leaves many unanswered.

First off, who built it? Masonry was not common in early North American cultures. Second up, what was it used for? As a single straight wall, it would keep nothing in or out, and it isn't particularly tall. A lot of good that would do anybody.

Some have suggested that it was used as an astronomical viewing device, as it runs due east and west. On the first day of spring and the first day of fall, it aligns with both sunrise and sunset. But that begs another question: why build a wall—wouldn't two properly aligned boulders work just as well?

Then again, could it be just a natural rock formation, its celestial orientation being a mere coincidence? Ponder all you like, but drop by at dawn or dusk on March 21 or September 21 and you'll no doubt conclude that something's going on here.

Blue Mounds State Park, RR 1, Luverne, MN 56156

(507) 283-1307

Hours: Daily 8 A.M.–4:30 P.M.

Cost: $4 daily permit

www.dnr.state.mn.us/state_parks/blue_mounds/index.html

Directions: North of town 4 miles, east of Rte. 75 on Rte. 20.

Saving Private Ryan

Though *Saving Private Ryan* was a realistic portrayal of fictional characters, it was based in part upon the real life of Francis L. Sampson, a Catholic priest with the 101st Airborne Division. Following the Normandy invasion, Father Sam was assigned to locate and evacuate Fritz Niland, a U.S. paratrooper. Though he didn't know it at the time, Niland had lost two of his brothers in separate European battles, and a third was missing in action in Burma. (It turns out, he survived.) Father Sampson found Niland and had him safely evacuated from Utah Beach, though not as dramatically as Tom Hanks did in the movie.

Unlike Hanks's character, Sampson wasn't given a ticket home after completing his mission. He advanced with the Allies until he was captured during the Battle of the Bulge. He spent the remainder of the war in a German POW camp.

Sampson stayed in the military through the Korean conflict and the Vietnam War. He was made the army's chief of chaplains in 1967. He died on January 28, 1996. Father Sam was buried in Luverne with family members who, strictly by coincidence, have the surname of Ryan.

St. Catherine Catholic Cemetery, James St. & Rte. 75, Luverne, MN 56156

(507) 283-8502

Hours: Daylight hours

Cost: Free

www.luvernemn.com

Directions: At the north end of town on Kings Ave. (Rte. 75).

Montevideo
¡Viva Uruguay!

José Artigas was the father of Uruguayan independence, but as far as anyone knows, never liberated a single Minnesotan. So why does this Midwestern town have a seven-foot statue honoring the South American hero? Think back to geography class: Montevideo is the capital of Uruguay . . . and just happens to be the sister city of Montevideo, Minnesota, which is also known as the Fiesta City.

Poor Uruguayan schoolchildren gathered their pesos to fund this 1949 statue by Juan Manuel Blanes. It stood downtown until 1967 when Lady Bird Johnson came to town to dedicate the Fiesta City Shelter on the brand-new Artigas Plaza.

Surprisingly, many residents and businesses seem unclear about the difference between Uruguay and Mexico, as evidenced by the number of sombreros painted on local signs. Still, international is international, and each year Montevideo celebrates Fiesta Days.

Jose Artigas Statue, Artigas Plaza, 100 N. First St., Montevideo, MN 56265

(800) 269-5527

Hours: Always visible

Cost: Free

www.montechamber.com

Directions: Four blocks north of the train tracks on First St.

New London
Little Crow Water-Ski Team

Not only did Minnesota give the world water-skiing (see page 140), but one of the world's great water-ski acts: the Little Crow Water Ski Team. Every Friday evening in summer the 60-member team puts on a performance along the Crow River that will have you on the edge of your picnic blanket. What they lack in 1950s sex-appeal (à la Cypress Gardens' spangle-suited maidens) and 1970s showmanship (à la the Skiing Elvi of Tommy Bartlett's Wisconsin Dells extravaganza), they more than make up in athleticism. Performers flip, jump, twirl, and stack themselves in every combination imaginable. The showstopper is the team's signature 42-person, 3-peak pyramid. They make it look easy, but please, do not try this at home.

Neer Park, 311 Second Ave. SE, PO Box 537, New London, MN 56273

(320) 354-5684

E-mail: littlecrowskiteam@yahoo.com

Hours: June–August, Friday 7:30 P.M.

Cost: Adults $4, Kids $1; Reserved seating $6

www.littlecrow.com

Directions: Two blocks north of Rte. 23 on Rte. 40.

New Ulm
Hermann the German and the Glockenspiel

New York has the Statue of Liberty. New Ulm has Hermann the German. Who's Hermann? None other than Hermann Armenius of Cherusci, the warrior who united the German people in A.D. 9 to defeat the advancing Romans at the Rhine River. Schnitzel mit spaghetti? Nein!

This Teutonic town in the upper Midwest erected a 32-foot copper statue to Hermann, designed by Julius Berndt and cast by Alfonso Pelzer, atop a 70-foot pedestal in 1897. Stairs lead to a platform just below the sword-swinging conqueror. The monument sits atop a bluff and offers an impressive view of the rest of the town.

Hermann Heights Park, Monument & Center Sts., New Ulm, MN 56073

(888) 4-NEW-ULM or (507) 359-8344

Hours: June–August (and during Oktoberfest), daily 10 A.M.–4 P.M.

Cost: Adults $1, Kids 50¢

www.newulm.com

Directions: Eight blocks southwest of Broadway (Rte. 15) on Center St. (Rte. 13).

From Hermann's perch, you can just make out the downtown's glockenspiel below the 37-bell carillon tower. Three times a day, every day, a dozen mechanical figures pop out of the clock on a town square to reenact this burg's colorful history. The Indians relinquish their land, homes are built, beer is brewed, and a couple dances the polka. Between Thanksgiving and New Year's Day, the characters are replaced with a robotic nativity, but no, the baby Jesus doesn't wear lederhosen.

Schonlau Park Plaza, 4th & Minnesota Sts., New Ulm, MN 56073

(507) 354-4217

Hours: Performances at Noon, 3 P.M., and 5 P.M.

Cost: Free

Directions: Just north of Broadway (Rte. 15) at 4th St.

SAUERKRAUT-LOVIN' BURG

New Ulm takes its German heritage very seriously, and there have been times when that got it into trouble. (The town was founded in 1854 by the German Land Society.) As the United States inched closer to entering World War I, New Ulm's mayor Louis Fritsche led locals in a declaration urging the United States not to get involved. It did anyway, a month later. Faced with fighting against their homeland, 6,000 local immigrants protested against the U.S. draft in Turner Park. State legislators were not sympathetic, and instead passed the Minnesota Sedition Act, which formed the Minnesota Commission of Public Safety. The goal was to ensure "100% patriotism." One of the commission's first actions was to remove Mayor Fritsche from office for anti-American activities, by order of Governor Burnquist.

Today, all seems to be forgotten. The town celebrates three annual festivals: Fasching, a sort of German Mardi Gras; Heritagefest, in July, honoring all things German; and, of course, Oktoberfest. At any of these festivals you're likely to run across the masked Narren (fools), or the even more frightening Gertie the Goose and the Heinzelmännchen Family, a group of gargantuan garden gnomes.

NEW GERMANY

New Germany's name was changed to Motordale during World War I.

NEW ULM

Wanda Gág, author and illustrator of the children's classic *Millions of Cats*, lived at 226 N. Washington Street in New Ulm.

Tippi Hedron was born Natalie Kay Hedron in New Ulm on January 19, 1935. Her family lived in nearby Lafayette.

North Redwood
Lemonade from Lemons

Richard Sears knew a good thing when it happened to him—even if it was a bad thing that happened to somebody else. At the age of 22 he was the North Redwood depot agent on the Minneapolis and St. Louis railroad line. Sometime in 1885, a box of watches arrived in his station after being refused by a jeweler in nearby Redwood Falls. Before shipping them back, Sears contacted the manufacturer and made an offer to buy the whole lot at $12 apiece. The manufacturer accepted.

Sears then used his position as an agent (with handy transportation and communication channels) to sell the watches to other agents for $14 each. Before long he was ordering even more half-priced watches to resell up and down the line, and not just to railroad employees. And he offered his buyers something nobody else did: a six-year guarantee. The R. W. Sears Watch Company was born!

Sears printed his first catalog in 1887 after he was reassigned to St. Paul. Soon after that he quit his railroad job and moved to Chicago where he met and partnered with watch repairman Alvah Roebuck. Their mail-order catalog eventually grew to be almost the size of the sleepy depot where it all started.

Route 101, North Redwood, MN 56283

No phone

Hours: Station torn down; tracks still visible

Cost: Free

Directions: Just east of the point where Rte. 101 crosses the railroad tracks.

PIPESTONE

Rumor has it that **Jesse James** buried between $25,000 and $100,000 on a farm near Pipestone. The farmer was believed to be in cahoots with the bandit and was run out of town before the money was recovered. It should still be there.

A "dummy" buffalo used in *Dances With Wolves* is on display at the Pipestone County Museum (113 S. Hiawatha Avenue).

Ear's to arms treaties!

Olivia
Big Ear of Corn

Wasn't this type of weapon banned under the START II Treaty? Well, somehow the folks in Olivia haven't heard the news. Sure, the 25-foot-tall ear of corn looks harmless enough, but rumor has it the green husk hides a Minuteman missile!

Consider these interesting "coincidences": Sometime in 1973, when ongoing arms control talks between the United States and the Soviet Union were thawing the Cold War, this big ear appeared atop a picnic shelter. Then superstar Olivia Newton-John showed up to dedicate the ear, all the way from Australia, and only asked for "fresh bread and two dozen ears of corn" for her trouble. Not only could she have demanded more, but there's no way she could eat that much!

And guess what's due east of this corn-loving town? South Dakota. And what's in South Dakota besides Mount Rushmore? That's right: hundreds of Minuteman missiles . . . or at least there used to be.

Memorial Park, 1600 W. Lincoln Ave., Olivia, MN 56277

No phone

Hours: Always visible

Cost: Free

olivia.mn.us/main.htm

Directions: On Rte. 212 (Lincoln Ave.) on the west side of town.

Ortonville
Paul Bunyan's Anchor

Exactly why this big lumberjack owned an anchor is not exactly clear. If you were to ask a historian, you'd probably learn it belonged to Mike Fink or Stormalong or another folk character who was a little more sailor-like. But this is Minnesota. Bunyan is what folks want. Bunyan is what folks get.

The 225,000-pound anchor was raised onto four (hopefully) sturdy pillars at a roadside pull-off near Big Stone Lake for the state's centennial in 1958. A single picnic table has been placed beneath the 112-ton slab of mahogany granite, which makes for a relaxing lunchtime stop, if the thought of being squished doesn't bother you.

Routes 12 & 75, Ortonville, MN 56278

(800) 568-5722

Hours: Always visible

Cost: Free

www.bigstonelake.com

Directions: On the southwest corner of the intersection of Rtes. 12 and 75, next to the Big Stone County Museum.

Dude—that's a wicked pipe!

Pipestone
Pipestone National Monument
and the World's Largest Peace Pipe

If you want to make a calumet (peace pipe) right, according to many Native American tribes, you've got to use pipestone. Trouble was, for many years the location of this quarry was, well, forgotten. But no more.

Pipestone is found only in this part of southwest Minnesota, which is why the land is protected today as a national monument. The carvable red clay's geologic name is catlinite (named for artist George Catlin) and can only be mined by Native Americans who perform the proper sacred ritual.

However, you don't have to travel very far off the monument before you see signs on local homes and businesses advertising pipestone on sale for three bucks a pound. This pipestone has been quarried from private land, and without the ritual extraction, it isn't true pipestone.

PO Box 727, Pipestone, MN 56164

(507) 825-5464

Hours: Daily 8 A.M.–8 P.M.

Cost: Adults $2, Kids (16 and under) Free

www.nps/gov/pipe

Directions: Rte. 75 north 0.5 miles from intersection with Rte. 23, west 0.5 miles.

. . . and would the town of Pipestone be able to show its civic face in Minnesota, Land of 10,000 Colossal Creations, were it not to build the World's Largest Peace Pipe? Surely not! A 30-foot-long calumet stands just outside the city's old Rock Island Depot. Rap on the tip and you'll know it's made of steel, not catlinite, but it should work just the same. And, dude, it has a bowl the size of a Weber grill!

400 N. Hiawatha Ave., Pipestone, MN 56164

(800) 336-6125

Hours: Always visible

Cost: Free

www.pipestone.mn.us or www.pipestoneminnesota.com

Directions: One block north of the railroad tracks, north of downtown at 4th St.

Redwood Falls
Minnesota Inventors Hall of Fame

Minnesota inventors have given the world a lot: Liquid Paper, Scotch-Gard, the heart-lung machine, sandpaper (see page 90 puffed rice, the Pied Piper rodent repeller, and Bounce dryer sheets, just to name a few. The Redwood County Museum has taken on the task of recognizing these creative accomplishments in a wing of its local historical society. The Minnesota Inventors Hall of Fame honors visionaries whose names you don't know, but whose inventions you do (although sometimes you won't know either).

The museum goes a step further by actually encouraging future inductees. Each June it hosts the Minnesota Inventors Congress. The event looks for all the world like a QVC casting call. How many electric egg-crackers and automated necktie racks does the world really need? Apparently, there's no limit.

Redwood County Museum, 507 Merton Dr., Redwood, MN 56283

(507) 637-3329

Hours: May–September, Wednesday–Sunday 1–5 P.M.

Cost: Free

Directions: West of town on Rte. 19.

Contact: Minnesota Inventors Congress, PO Box 71, Redwood Falls, MN 56283

(800) INVENT-1

www.invent1.org

SACRED HEART

The town of Sacred Heart was named for a local trader, Charles Patterson, who wore a "sacred hat" given to him by the Dakota. Nobody seems to know how the name was altered.

SLEEPY EYE

Sleepy Eye was named after local Sisseton Sioux chief, Ish-tak-ha-ba, whose saggy eyelids the settlers thought looked sleepy. He is buried near the town depot (1st Avenue N and Oak Street).

WATKINS

Senator Eugene McCarthy was born in Watkins on March 29, 1916.

WAVERLY

Waverly was the hometown of **Senator/Vice President Hubert Humphrey**.

Sanborn
The Sod House on the Prairie B&B

Ah, the good ol' days! They were . . . dirty . . . or, more accurately, soddy. Yep, when pioneers decided to farm the treeless prairie, there was precious little to use as a building material. Except, of course, the very ground they were standing upon. Cut into bricks, the root-filled sod was placed grass-side down to construct the walls of a traditional sod house. On the roof, sod was placed grass-side up, making for an interesting front lawn.

If you want to get a firsthand look at life in a soddy, why not spend the night in one: the Sod House on the Prairie B&B. It was built in 1987 by Stan McCone. He's added a few "modern" features, like a wooden floor and a subroof, and plastered walls, but it's still an authentic pioneer experience, minus the grasshopper plagues, cholera, and Indian uprisings. The whole structure is surrounded by restored grassland. There's no running water, no electricity, and if you want to stay up past sundown, you'll need to light the oil lamps. And when nature calls, there's a sod outhouse.

12598 Magnolia Ave., Sanborn, MN 56083

(507) 723-5138

Hours: Call for reservations; Tours April–October, call ahead

Cost: $100/couple, $130/3 people, $10/additional guest to 5; Tours $3

www.bbonline.com/mn/sodhouse

Directions: South of Rte. 14, one road east of Rte. 71.

Walnut Grove
Laura Ingalls Wilder Dugout and Museum

One of the strangest endings to a television series was the final episode of *Little House on the Prairie*. When greedy land barons acquired the land beneath Walnut Grove, Pa talks the citizens into blowing the town to bits. One by one, they detonate every home and business (except the church) while the land barons watch, then Pa leads the bombers out of town singing "Onward, Christian Soldiers."

Well, the episode was a shock to readers of Laura Ingalls Wilder's books, as it was to the folks of Walnut Grove, which is still very much a town in southwest Minnesota. The show's final plot twist was in fact the warped final tantrum of creator Michael Landon, captured on film. Landon found out that his show had been canceled in 1983 when he read the news in *Variety*. He marched out to the town set he'd made famous and reduced it to kindling while the cameras rolled. He then wrote a script where NBC executives were thinly disguised as the ruthless land barons. Now that's subtle.

The real Ingalls family faced more hardship than Landon ever did. The family moved to the area in 1874, when Laura was seven, to homestead north of town. Pa's dream of becoming a wheat farmer was gobbled up by swarms of grasshoppers. In Walnut Grove, Laura met her nemesis, Nellie Owens (not Oleson!), daughter of the town's general store owner. A son, Charles Frederic, was born here, but "Freddie" died before his first birthday while the defeated family was en route to Burr Oak, Iowa. When they returned a year later, Mary caught scarlet fever and went blind. The family left for good in 1880. The whole tale was captured by Wilder in her 1937 classic, *On the Banks of Plum Creek*, though she glossed over much of the rough stuff.

Ingalls Family Dugout, Gordon Farm, Rte. 5, Walnut Grove, MN 56180
No phone
Hours: May–October, daily dawn–dusk
Cost: $3/car
Directions: North of town 1.5 miles on Rte. 5.

Wilder may have renamed Walnut Grove as Plum Creek in her book, but the folks here knew the truth. The Ingalls dugout, washed away in a 1920s flood, is little more than an indentation on the riverbank west of town. The two-story home Pa built on the farm is also long gone, but it stood near the barn on the Gordon farm, the barn you'll pass on the way to the dugout.

In Walnut Grove, you'll find Pa's church bell on the English Lutheran Church (450 Wiggans Street)—he donated $26.15 to the congregation for its purchase, even though his kids were without shoes. The church where it originally hung, the Union Congregational Church (southeast corner of 5th and Bedal Streets) is now a private home. The Walnut Grove school that the girls attended also stands, but it too is a private residence (northeast corner of 4th and Washington Streets).

At the town's Wilder Museum you'll see the Wilder family Bible, an original quilt, and Michael Landon's gun from the TV series. If you're an NBC executive, you should keep it to yourself.

Laura Ingalls Wilder Museum, PO Box 58, 330 Eighth St., Walnut Grove, MN 56180

(888) 528-7268 or (866) LAURA-43 or (507) 859-2358

E-mail: liw@rconnect.com

Hours: June–August, daily 10 A.M.–6 P.M.; May, September, Monday–Saturday 10 A.M.–
   5 P.M., Sunday Noon–5 P.M.; October, April, Monday–Saturday 10 A.M.–4 P.M., Sunday
   Noon–4 P.M.; November–March, call ahead

Cost: Adults $3, Kids (6–12) $1

www.walnutgrove.org

Directions: On the corner of 8th and Ingalls Sts., just south of the train tracks.

In the summers, Walnut Grove puts on the Wilder Pageant, an epic saga of
the travails of the Ingalls family. The elaborate outdoor theater is located
on the banks of the same Plum Creek that passes the Ingalls dugout.

Wilder Pageant, PO Box 313, Walnut Grove, MN 56180

(888) 859-3102 or (507) 859-2174

Hours: Last three weekends in July, 9 P.M.; gates open 7 P.M.

Cost: Seats $6–$8

Directions: One mile west of town.

MORE FOR LAURA LOVERS

In May 1890, four years after **Laura Ingalls** married Almanzo Wilder
in De Smet, South Dakota, the couple moved to Spring Valley in
southeastern Minnesota with their young daughter, Rose. They moved
in with Almanzo's parents, who had lived in the area since the 1870s.
A year later, in October 1891, the trio left Spring Valley for Florida.
All that is left of the Wilder farm is a stone-walled barn on Tracey
Road, two blocks west of Route 63 on the north end of town. (It is
privately owned, so view it from the street.)

WILLMAR

A 17-foot-tall statue of Chief Kandiyohi stands in front of the Kandiyohi
County Courthouse (5th Street and Becker Avenue) in Willmar. Though it
appears to be made of gold, it is actually painted fiberglass.

Willmar
Mikkelson's Boat Museum

If you've never heard of the Falls Flyer, you're obviously not a boating enthusiast. That's like a car buff saying, "What's a Lamborghini?" There were only about 200 Falls Flyers ever manufactured by the Larson Boat Works between 1939 and 1960, but their reputation for craftsmanship earned them the nickname "the Jaguar of boats." Falls Flyers were named in honor of Little Falls's Charles Lindbergh. They were sleek—many looked like a cross between a banana and a flying saucer—powerful, and dependable.

Paul Mikkelson owns more Falls Flyers than any human on the planet— more than 25—and most can be seen at this museum on a rotating basis. He's got the only two split-cockpit inboards, and the only single-cockpit inboard Speedster the company ever made, named the *Boondoggle*.

To get to these wonderful watercraft you must first walk past Mikkelson's 500-piece collection of toy boats, all carefully displayed in glass cases, and a hundred or so restored outboard motors. Enthusiasts will find Mikkelson an unstumpable answer-man of boating trivia, so if you have a question, ask away. And if you have one of the few remaining Falls Flyers, know that you'll make a friend for life.

418 Benson Ave. SE, Willmar, MN 56201

(320) 231-0384

Hours: Saturday 9 A.M.–4 P.M., and by appointment

Cost: Adults $6

www.fallsflyer.com

Directions: Two blocks east of Rte. 71 (Memorial Parkway), one block north of Rte. 12.

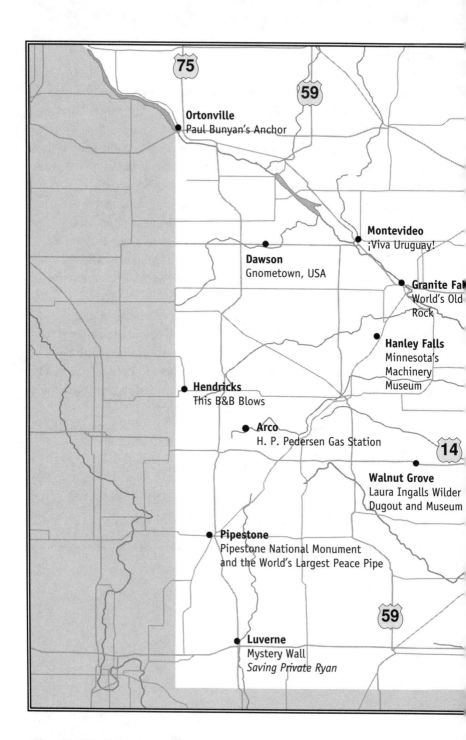

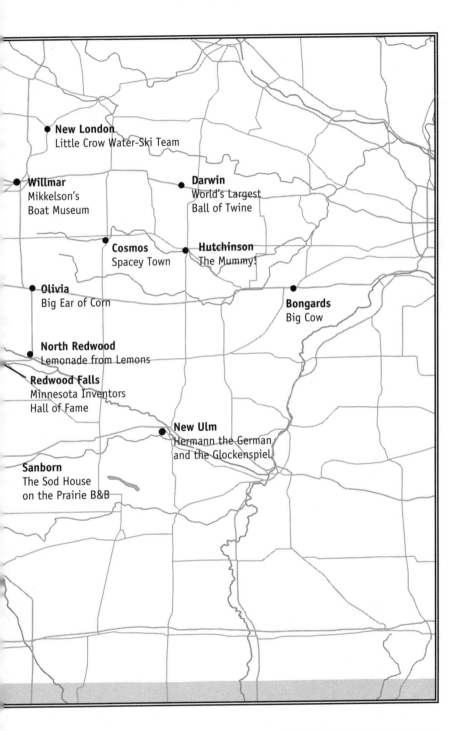

4

THE SOUTHEAST

*F*illmore County, in far southeast Minnesota, is a true oddball. Here, in the Land of 10,000 Lakes, you can't find a single lake. Not one! Yet it's hardly the strangest place in these parts. Head toward Iowa from the Twin Cities and you're likely to encounter the Jolly Green Giant, a Spam museum, or scarier still, the Abominable Snowman!

Don't worry, the locals will protect you. Ask Jesse James or Cole Younger, two bandits who met their match in the good citizens of Northfield. The region is also home to the World's Largest Revolver, a museum with the only complete collection of Winchester firearms anywhere, and Cabela's, where ammo is always well stocked.

There are plenty of odd things, too, for those not interested in weaponry. Southeast Minnesota is home to two fine toy museums, a two-story jewel box, and a B&B where every visitor gets a cuddly-wuddly kitty cat.

Can you think of a broader spectrum of vacation possibilities?

Albert Lea
Itasca Rock Garden

Hidden away on a country road, in a town long since swallowed by its neighbor, Albert Lea, are the remnants of Minnesota's most elaborate folk art environment: the Itasca Rock Garden. It was started in 1925 by John Christensen using the stones he'd collected on his trips across America. Rather than make rock beds, he embedded the stones in the sides of bridges and benches and planters. The garden grew, and Christensen erected a large castle in the center of the space, surrounded by a moat and tiny homes guarded by troll statues.

Eventually, the project spilled into the basement of the Christensen home, where he built a pool and year-round greenhouse. He didn't stop until 1938, and a year later he died. The current owners have plans to restore the gardens to their original splendor, but until they do, the site is off-limits to the public. However, feel free to admire them from the nearby road.

2129 Itasca Rd., Albert Lea, MN 56007
Private phone
Hours: Always visible; view from street
Cost: Free
Directions: Exit I-90 on Rte. 13 heading south, immediately turn east on Rte. 101, follow the road to the left at the Y, turn right on Bluegrass Rd., then look to your right as the road bends to become Itasca Rd.

ALBERT LEA

Marion Ross was born in Albert Lea on October 25, 1928.

Albert Lea was chosen as the county seat of Freeborn County in 1860 following a horse race between Albert Lea and Itasca, which had been organized to establish a winner.

Rock star **Eddie Cochran** was born in Albert Lea. The town celebrates Eddie Cochran Days each June.

SPAM . . . This is your life!!!
Photo by author, courtesy of the Spam Museum

Austin
Spam Museum

The Spam Museum isn't one of those museums you should drive out of your way to see—it's one you should drive *way out of your way* to see! Even if you're not a meat-in-a-can fan, it is impossible not to be swept up in the goofy, giddy enthusiasm that permeates this museum. When you step through the door you're greeted by the mighty Wall of Spam constructed with 3,390 (empty) cans. A rotating globe indicates Spam's worldwide appeal. Visitors are asked to wait in the Cyberdiner for the next showing of *Spam: A Love Story*, the museum's introduction to the product that made it rich. Enter the Hormel Theater through the doors with piggy snout handles, and let your Spam education begin.

Spam was not the first meat product Hormel ever made. The company was founded in 1892, but Spam wasn't invented until 1937. "Spam" is a contraction for "spiced ham," a name dreamed up by Kenneth Daigneau, which won him $100. (Oddly, the food contains little ham and few spices—it's made mostly of pig shoulders.) Had Spam not hit the market just after World War II erupted, it is unlikely that it would be as popular as it is today. American GIs were fed a healthy diet of the stuff, and when they returned home they sang the praises of their mess hall favorite. (Well, it wasn't *every* GI's favorite, but soldiers did admire the meat's wartime mascot, Slammin' Spammy, the bomb-throwing, Nazi-killing pig.)

After passing through the museum's historical exhibits—including a puppet version of *This Is Your Life* hosted by Gracie Allen—you'll learn how Spam is produced, packaged, and marketed. Try your hand as an assembly-line worker, cramming Spam-shaped beanbags into real cans while a clock ticks. It's just like Lucy and the candy conveyor, only you might not want to cram these things into your mouth. Step into the Changing Marketplace exhibit, a minigrocery bulging with every Hormel product imaginable, including Dinty Moore Beef Stew. And just to be sure you've been paying attention, test your wits with *The Spam Exam*, a multimedia quiz show hosted by Al Franken—you're the contestant!

Like most corporate museums, this one dumps out into an elaborate gift shop. T-shirts, plush toys, jewelry, clocks, cookbooks, mugs, snow globes, golf balls, and fly swatters. They've even got flip-flops that leave the Spam logo in the sand as you stroll along the beach. Loaded with shopping bags full of Spamabilia, you exit down Spamburger Alley past a 17.5-foot spatula and a 25-square-foot Spam slice, enough to make 4,800 normal-size sandwiches.

If you want to keep on a Spam high, there are several sights around Austin. Founder George Hormel is buried in Oakwood Cemetery (1800 Fourth Street NW) in the family plot. The Hormel mansion is located at 208 Fourth Avenue NW. Stop by the Hormel Institute, one of the nation's leading lipid (fat) research centers, where work is being done to combat heart disease and cancer. Or take a cruise on the *Spamtown Belle*, a paddle-wheeler on East Side Lake. Come to Austin on Fourth of July weekend and you can attend the town's three-day Spam Jamboree, complete with a three-mile run, a gooey Spam Gelatin Jump, Spam carving contests, and a Spam Cook-Off where you'll see Spam kabobs, Spam spring rolls, Spam pizza, Spam Caesar salad, and more.

1937 Spam Blvd. (Main St.), Austin, MN 55912

(800) LUV-SPAM or (507) 437-5100

Spam Jamboree: (800) 444-5713

Hours: Monday–Saturday 10 A.M.–5 P.M., Sunday Noon–4 P.M.

Cost: Free

www.hormel.com

Spam Appreciation Society: www.spam69.demon.co.uk/spam.htm

Directions: Sixth St. East Exit from I-90, south to the Hormel plant, follow the road to the right; the museum is just ahead.

SPAM TRIVIA

★ Spam is uncooked when it enters the can, but the sterilization process takes care of that.

★ The title of Hormel's company newsletter is *Squeal*.

★ Spam admirer John Nagamichi Cho has collected more than 17,000 Spam haikus, named Spam-kus (pemtropics.mit.edu/~jcko/spam/).

★ In 2002, Hormel produced its 6 billionth can of Spam.

★ Spam can be used to polish furniture.

ALBERT LEA

A replica of Copenhagen's **Little Mermaid** statue rests on a rock in Albert Lea's Fountain Lake.

BLUE EARTH

Blue Earth is the birthplace of the ice cream sandwich.

Head's up!

Belle Plaine
Two-Story Outhouse

The cold Minnesota winters have caused many citizens of this great state to take drastic action. Consider the years when most homes did not have indoor plumbing and a trip to the outhouse could invite serious frost-bite. And who wants to keep a chamber pot around the house until a spring thaw?

Enter the solution: the two-story outhouse! Oh, some laughed at first when the owners built the five-seat structure in 1871. It was attached to the large home by a second-story covered skyway, allowing those who used it to avoid the deep snow and cold winds as they answered the call of nature. Who was laughing *then*?

Thanks to the efforts of historic preservationists, Belle Plaine's most famous piece of architecture is still in fine working order, though you are not allowed to use it during the tour.

Hooper-Bowler-Hillstrom House, 410 N. Cedar, Belle Plaine, MN 56011

Contact: Belle Plaine Historical Society, PO Box 73, Belle Plaine, MN 56011

(952) 873-6408 or (952) 873-4433

Hours: Always visible; house tour Sunday 1–4 P.M.

Cost: Free; house tour $2/person

www.frontiernet.net/~bellepln/Local_Attractions.htm

Directions: One block west of Rte. 25 (Walnut St.), two blocks north of Rte. 6 (Main St.), at Court St.

CHATFIELD
It is illegal to cross-dress in public in Chatfield.

CONCEPTION
The town of Conception is named for a local church, the Church of the Immaculate Conception.

ELGIN
The gravestone above the **Robert H. Hallenbeck** family in the Elgin City Cemetery reads, "None of us ever voted for Roosevelt or Truman." Chances are, they never will.

FARIBAULT
A white, rectangular UFO was spotted over Faribault by **Dick Feichtinger** on April 2, 1991. It hovered all day, and later turned red and green.

Ho! Ho! Ho!

Blue Earth
Jolly Green Giant Statue

The nation's most famous (and most friendly) giant resides in a town not much bigger than he is. But the people of Blue Earth have big ideas, as witnessed by the fact that they shelled out $43,000 for this 55-foot-high fiberglass statue in September 1978. The erection coincided with the completion of I-90 when the east and west arms of the northern interstate were joined just outside town. Miss America and Miss Minnesota dropped by to see it go up, and the tourists have been coming ever since.

The Jolly Green Giant started in the late 1920s as the mascot of the Blue Earth Canning Company, which was later absorbed by Le Sueur's Minnesota Valley Canning Company, which has since been swallowed up by a series of multinational food conglomerates over the years.

But the giant remains . . . nobody dares mess with him. He's a hefty four tons, his smile is four feet wide, and his six-foot elfin slippers are a size 78.

Jolly Green Giant Statue Park, Rte. 169 & Green Giant Ave., Blue Earth, MN 56013

(507) 526-2916

Hours: Always visible

Cost: Free

chamber.blue-earth.mn.us

Directions: Exit Rte. 169 south from I-90.

Good Thunder
Elegant Elevator

Almost every Minnesota town has a grain elevator, but few have as elegant an elevator as Good Thunder. Back in 1987, the town decided to spruce up the structure on Main Street and hired artist Ta-Coumba Aiken for the job. (It had not been used as much as it had before the Milwaukee Wisconsin Railroad decided to take Good Thunder off its service route.) The long-term goal of the project was to attract other artists to the community and perhaps give a shot in the arm to the sagging local economy. It didn't work, but the mural still attracts tourists.

Aiken's 1,100-gallons-of-paint mural depicts people and scenes from the area's history. Most prominent is a 40-foot portrait of Wa-kin-yan-was-te, the Ho Chunk (Winnebago) chief whose name translated roughly as "Good Thunder." It also features such former local luminaries as Richard Houk, the town's first surveyor; John and Loretta Graham, the first postmaster and his wife; and Robbert Stratton, a casualty of World War II and the man whose name is on the local VFW post. Never heard of any of them? That's not the point. Do you really know who Mona Lisa was, or that sour old couple in *American Gothic*? Exactly.

Main & Front Sts., Good Thunder, MN 56037

No phone

Hours: Always visible

Cost: Free

Directions: At the corner of Rtes. 10 (Main St.) and Front St.

Harmony
Harmony Toy Museum

Visitors enter the Harmony Toy Museum past a floor-to-ceiling wall of thrift-store art, the kind that looks like paint-by-numbers but isn't. This is their first clue that this museum isn't the Smithsonian. Turn the corner and you enter the mind and mania of Wesley Idso, collector and curator of the curious.

Idso is one of those people who can't throw anything away, yet he also feels compelled to share it all with the world. In 1994, he packed up his collection of kids' toys (some of which he'd made, but most leftovers from his six kids) and moved them into a storefront on Main Street. Like a gas, the number of artifacts expanded to fill the space. The collection ballooned to more than 5,000 items. Idso installed a living room smack-dab in the middle of the museum so visitors would feel free to sit among the many wonders. Clocks and calendars. Newspapers and movie posters. Buttons and bottles. And toys, toys, toys, toys, toys, toys, toys. If you're a suburban family with a basement, you'll feel right at home.

30 S. Main St., Harmony, MN 55939

(507) 867-3380

Hours: May–October, Monday–Saturday 9 A.M.–4 P.M., Sunday 11 A.M.–4 P.M.

Cost: Free, donations accepted

www.harmony.mn.us

Directions: One block south of Center St. on Rte. 139 (Main St.).

Slim's Woodshed

You could almost say that Stanley "Slim" Maroushek was destined to open a woodcarving museum. As a child he lived in Spillville, Iowa, and did odd jobs for the Bily Brothers. The brothers are famous for carving dozens of elaborate mechanical clocks that can still be found in their hometown.

Slim was given small carved toys by the Bilys, and it started a lifelong fascination with the craft. (Unfortunately, Slim's Bily pieces are long gone.)

Slim started as a collector, amassing more than 1,700 carvings from across the globe. Most of them are on display in this one-room museum. Some are fairly common, like saddle-weary cowboys in 10-gallon hats, but most have some sort of unique feature. If you don't take the tour, you won't be able to see the hidden whiskey flask in the troll statue or the inner workings of the mechanical bottle-stopper heads from Italy as they tip back a drink or two. The museum's got Philippine monkeys carved from coconuts, a four-foot movable Malaysian snake, a cypress knee Santa, and Pigasus (a flying oinker). Most are made of wood, but a few are carved from camel bones and water buffalo horns. At the center of the room is a two-ring circus made by 23 members of the Caricature Carvers of America. Each carver was given a different circus act to portray, and all were arranged in and around a big top tent—trapeze artists, knife throwers, a human cannonball, buck-toothed carneys, a sanitation engineer (scoop in hand), ticket takers, Mr. Tubs the gorilla, and lots and lots of clowns.

Slim has big plans for the future. In the next five years he hopes to erect a replica of a Depression-era hobo camp in a town park, complete with life-size wooden hobos.

160 First St. NW, PO Box 594, Harmony, MN 55939

(507) 886-3114

E-mail: slim_ws@means.net

Hours: May–December, Monday–Saturday 9 A.M.–5 P.M., Sunday Noon–5 P.M.; January–April, Tuesday–Saturday 9 A.M.–5 P.M., Sunday Noon–5 P.M.

Cost: Adults $3.50, Seniors (65+) $2, Kids (6–18) $2

www.website.com/slimswoodshed

Directions: One block north of Center St., one block west of Main St. (Rte. 139).

LA CRESENT
La Cresent calls itself the Apple Capital of the World.

A hunter near La Cresent stumbled across a Bigfoot in 1968; both hunter and creature ran screaming in opposite directions.

Harmony and Spring Valley
A Couple of Caves

The divergent tales of Niagara Cave and Mystery Cave should serve as a warning for all those who dare "improve" America's roadside attractions by making them less kitschy and more educational. Years ago, both caverns were hokey fun for travelers looking for an underground adventure. Then something went terribly, terribly wrong.

But first the good news. Harmony's Niagara Cave has retained its old-style goofy atmosphere. The caves were discovered in 1924 by a farmer who went looking for his lost pigs. He located them in what is today the Reception Room. But there was much more to this hole in the ground than an old pig trap. Deep beneath the surface you can be married in its 10-seat Crystal Wedding Chapel. Only 300 couples have so far shared this honor over the years. The chapel sits adjacent to the three-tier Wedding Cake. Though it stays chilled by the 48°F cavern air, you still can't eat it—it's a stalagmite!

And there's more. Check out the Liberty Bell formation, complete with a crack. See the impressive Grand Dad Stalactite, or Paul Bunyan's Bed; or toss your pocket change in the Wishing Well. And 150 feet beneath the surface you'll see a 60-foot waterfall from a footbridge spanning the pig-swallowing chasm. Talk about fun!

Niagara Cave, Niagara Cave Rd., PO Box 444, Harmony, MN 55939
(800) 837-6606 or (507) 886-6606
Hours: May–September, daily 9:30 A.M.–5:30 P.M.; October–April, Saturday–Sunday 10 A.M.–4:30 P.M.
Cost: Adults $8, Seniors (65+) $7, Teens (13–17) $8, Kids (4–12) $4.50
www.niagaracave.com
Directions: Drive two miles south of Harmony on Rte. 139, turn west on Rte. 30 (Niagara Cave Rd.); the cave is two miles ahead.

. . . and then there's Mystery Cave. Discovered in 1937, it was at one time very similar to Niagara. Carved by the Root River, it has two magnificent underground lakes and dozens of exposed fossils such as 18- to 20-foot cephalopods, ancestors of today's octopus and squid.

As Minnesota's longest cave, Mystery's all very interesting, but it's also understated. The caverns are maintained by Forestville State Park, which has chosen to run the attraction as an *educational* cave. No goofy names for the formations. Latin names on all the fossils. And in 1989 the park ripped out the gaudy 12-foot statue of Chief Decorah that guarded the cave entrance and donated it to the town of Spring Valley. Today the 1940 concrete creation of Halvor Landsverk stands next to the town's tourist information hut (Route 63/16), and it has been painted in a monochrome tan. Some improvement.

Forestville State Park, Route 2, PO Box 128, Preston, MN 55965

(507) 937-3251

E-mail: warren.netherton@dnr.state.mn.us

Hours: April–May and September–October, Saturday–Sunday 10 A.M.–5 P.M.; June–
August, daily 10 A.M.–5 P.M.

Cost: Adults $7, Kids (5–12) $4 with $4 state park pass

www.dnr.state.mn.us/state_parks/forestville_mystery_cave/index.html

Directions: Four miles south of Rte. 16 on Rte. 5, following the signs.

Kellogg
L.A.R.K. Toys

Have you ever wanted to chuck it all and follow your dream? Well, Donn Kreofsky has a lot more courage than you—he actually did it. He was an art professor at two local colleges when he decided to start his own toy-making enterprise. What started as a small-time operation has grown to a large business, though it still retains its old-world charm. L.A.R.K. manufactures more than 100,000 wooden toys each year, and each one is made with tender loving care.

The same cannot be said, however, for many of the specimens in the company's toy museum. This doesn't mean they aren't *fun*; they're just not handmade. Slinkys and action figures and hula hoops line the shelves—for most adults it's a trip down memory lane. L.A.R.K. also has a 26-character carousel. The animals are better than what you would expect; you can ride an ostrich, a fish, a river otter, a dragon, a reindeer, or a giraffe with orangutans hanging from its neck.

L.A.R.K. Toys, Inc., RR 2, PO Box 5, Kellogg, MN 55945

(507) 767-3387

Hours: Monday–Friday, 9 A.M.–5 P.M., Saturday–Sunday 10 A.M.–5 P.M.

Cost: Free

www.larktoys.com

Directions: West on Rte. 18 from Rte. 61, then south on Lark Lane.

Lake City
Birthplace of Waterskiing

Xtreme sports fans might think they invented daredevil sports behavior in the 1990s. Not so. Way back in 1922, 18-year-old Ralph Samuelson was looking for a little excitement in his hometown of Lake City, so he strapped two wooden slats on his feet and got a friend with a fast boat to pull him around on Lake Pepin. He took more than a few spills because he first tried it with downhill skis, but after perfecting a wider rein-forced, curved ski, he was skipping across the waves, this time on his feet—and waterskiing was born!

Folks from all around came to watch Samuelson, "Daredevil of the Waves." He was all too happy to live up to his nickname. He was the first person to ride on a single ski. Before long, he was being towed behind airborne seaplanes. The town built a bandstand so people could make a day of it, listening to music while that nut kid risked his neck.

The town has never forgotten Samuelson, and has erected a small shrine to his achievement in the local chamber of commerce. Somebody found an old pair of water skis with the initials *RWS* on them. Whether or not they were Ralph's, and whether or not they were the original skis, is still open for debate. But one thing there's no argument about in these parts: Ralph Samuelson was one crazy-ass kid, and the world's a better place because of it.

Lake City Chamber of Commerce, 212 S. Washington St., Lake City, MN 55401

(800) 369-4123 or (651) 345-4123

E-mail: lcchamber@mr.net

Hours: Monday–Friday 9 A.M.–5 P.M.

Cost: Free

www.lakecitymn.org

Directions: One block north of Rte. 61, one block east of Lyon Ave. (Rte. 63).

LaSalle
The Younger Brothers Are Captured

All of southern Minnesota was alerted to the bank raid in Northfield on September 7, 1876 (see page 147), and posses were formed to track down the fleeing robbers. At one time, more than 1,000 men had enlisted to find the gang, many no doubt inspired by the reward that had been offered.

Somewhere along the way, Jesse and Frank James parted company with the Youngers and Charlie Pitts. Teenager Oscar Sorbell spotted the Youngers on September 21 and raced to nearby Madelia to warn the town. A posse tracked the four fugitives to a thicket just south of present-day LaSalle. Charlie Pitts was killed in the shoot-out that followed. The Youngers survived, albeit somewhat bullet-ridden; Cole had been shot 11 times, James 5 times, and Bob only once, but in the chest.

The Youngers were brought to Madelia where they were held at the Flanders Hotel (W. Main Street). Unlike the citizens of Northfield, the folks here fawned over the shackled Youngers, sending them flowers and listening to their stories through the windows. The trio was soon moved to Fairbault where they received similar treatment . . . and more than 4,000 visitors. Cole Younger was asked who had shot Heywood, but his vapid response to authorities was obnoxiously self-serving: "Be true to your friends if the Heavens fall." Oh, how noble. (To follow the rest of this story, turn to page 147.)

Route 3, LaSalle, MN 56056

No phone

Hours: Always visible

Cost: Free

Directions: South of Rte. 22, just south of the Watonwan River bridge.

LAKE CITY

The steamer *Seawing* capsized on Lake Pepin off Lake City on July 13, 1890, killing 98 passengers.

Lake City celebrates Johnny Appleseed Days each October where the Unusual Vegetable Contest is the big event.

Le Sueur
Le Sueur Museum
Sure, there must be a lot of other things that happened around here that might be interesting, but what you really want to see at this local history museum is its Green Giant Room. In it you'll find the history of a small-town corn-canning operation that ballooned into one of the nation's largest vegetable distributors.

The company was started by the Cosgrove family in 1903 as the Minnesota Valley Canning Company. It began featuring the Jolly Green Giant on its packaging in 1928; the gargantuan idea came from the advertising firm of Leo Burnett. The company became so tied in with its trademark that in 1950 it changed its name to the Green Giant Company. (The Minnesota River Valley, however, has still not been changed to the Valley of the Jolly Green Giant.)

Pillsbury bought out the operation in 1987 and moved the headquarters to Minneapolis. Before leaving, the company donated its archives to the local museum, which provided the seed for the Green Giant Room. Here you'll learn why the giant wears that red scarf and where Little Green Sprout came from.

709 N. 2nd St., Le Sueur, MN 56058

(507) 665-2050

Hours: September–May, Tuesday–Thursday 8 A.M.–Noon, 1–4:30 P.M.; June–August, daily 1–4:30 P.M.

Cost: Free, donations encouraged

home.le-sueur.mn.us or www.greengiant.com

Directions: One block east of Rte. 112 at Pine St.

Mankato
Largest Legal Execution in the USA
Mankato holds the dubious distinction of hosting the largest legal execution ever carried out on American soil. On December 26, 1862, 38 Sioux warriors were executed at the same time for the collective murder of 800-some Minnesota settlers.

The hostilities began during the summer drought of 1862 when the starving Sioux asked trader Andrew Myrick for credit to buy food. "If your people are hungry, let them eat grass, or their own dung," Myrick responded. Bad answer. On August 17, four Sioux warriors killed the five-member Baker family near Acton for some eggs—and the war was on.

Little Crow was drafted to lead the fight against the settlers, though he accepted it reluctantly. Warriors burned the town of New Ulm to the ground on August 19, killing 66 residents. There was another battle four days later. By the time the insurrection was put down by Colonel Henry Sibley and the state militia on September 23 at Wood Lake, hundreds from both sides had died all across south-central Minnesota. One of the casualties was Andrew Myrick; he was found with his mouth stuffed with grass. It could have been worse—it could have been his own dung.

Two thousand Sioux, mostly women and children, were rounded up and imprisoned in Mankato. After hasty court-martials, 307 were sentenced to death. President Abraham Lincoln commuted the sentences of all but 38 who were simultaneously hanged on an elaborate gallows on the day after Christmas. After they were buried, Dr. W. W. Mayo, founder of the Mayo Clinic, unearthed the bodies and used them for his own medical research. A historical plaque long marked the location near downtown Mankato. A riverfront park dedicated to reconciliation has now been placed on the site.

Reconciliation Park, Main St. & Riverfront Dr., Mankato, MN 56003

No phone

Hours: Always visible

Cost: Free

www.mankato.com

Directions: At the corner of Riverfront Dr. and Main St., just north of the depot.

MANKATO
Red cars are illegal in Mankato.

MEDFORD
Jerry Kay and his wife spotted a UFO landing on a Medford football field on November 2, 1975.

MONTGOMERY
Montgomery calls itself the Kolacky Capital of the World. The town celebrates Kolacky Days each July to honor the Bohemian pastry.

World's Largest Revolver

Believe it or not, the World's Largest Revolver has nothing to do with the Sioux uprising of 1862. In fact, it wasn't built until the 1940s. Unlike many of Minnesota's oversized objects, this 8.5-foot, 175-pound six-shooter is made of neither fiberglass nor cement, but steel and wood, just like a real gun. Nobody has ever fired it because nobody thought to build the World's Largest Bullets. The gun hangs in the window of a gun shop disguised as a museum . . . or is that the other way around?

Guns of the Pioneers, Old West Gun Shop & Museum, 300 Belgrade, Mankato, MN 56003

(507) 344-4440

Hours: Always visible; call for museum hours (sporadic)

Cost: Free

Directions: At Range St., one block west of Rte. 169 at the bridge.

NORTHFIELD
Northfield is the City of Cows, Colleges, and Contentment.

OWATONNA
Owatonna claims to be the Butter Capital of the World.

Actor **E. G. Marshall** was born in Owatonna on June 18, 1910. He chose to be called by his initials because too many people called him Edna, mispronouncing his real first name: Edda (Gunnar).

On Christmas 1880, the Dimant family of Owatonna were besieged by a doorbell that would not stop ringing. Shortly thereafter, a cylindrical glass "bomb" exploded in their parlor, causing Mrs. Dimant to pass out. Nobody seemed to know how it got there. . . .

An endangered species.

North Mankato
Happy Chef

There was a time when the Midwest was populated with an army of
Happy Chefs, each one guarding a roadside eatery with an upraised

spoon. If you touched a button on the base of a Happy Chef, he'd tell you a happy story about the restaurant chain.

But things recently haven't been so great for the 20-foot guys in the white hats. One by one they've gone silent, been kidnapped by drunken high schoolers, or both. They're a vanishing breed, like the passenger pigeons of a century ago. Though the restaurant chain still exists, statues like the one in North Mankato are a rarity. (You can find another in Marshall, on Route 19.)

Today, his Cheshire cat–like grin seems almost sinister, the twisted grimace of a downsized worker backed into a corner, his spoon his only weapon. Better see him while you still can, but for heaven's sake, don't upset him.

Happy Chef Restaurant, Rtes. 14 & 169, North Mankato, MN 56001

(507) 388-2953

Hours: Always visible

Cost: Free

Directions: Just north of Rte. 14 on Rte. 169.

ROCHESTER

Nineteen miles southeast of Rochester along Route 52, heading toward Chatfield, one of **Ma Barker**'s gang buried $100,000 in ransom money. It is still somewhere along a fence line beside the road.

A Bigfoot jogged past the headlights of a car near Rochester on December 14, 1979: Some think it was the same creature spotted 10 years earlier crouching over a dead rabbit near the same spot.

VIOLA

Minnesota may be the Gopher State, but that doesn't prevent the town of Viola from hosting the annual Gopher Count each June. If there is truth in advertising, this is more of a Dead Gopher Count; organizers pay $1.25 for each pair of front legs from these crop-ruinin', hole-diggin' varmints.

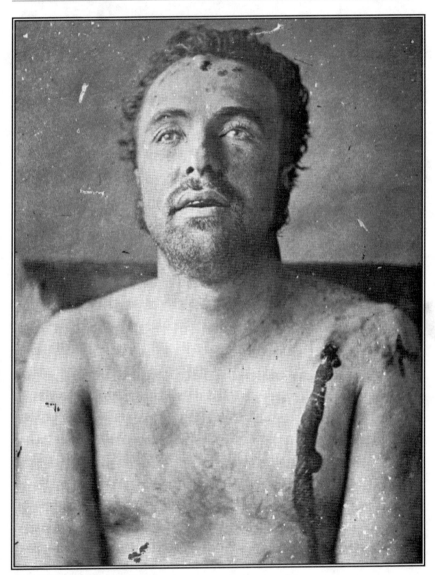

Clell Miller has seen better days.
Courtesy of the Northfield Historical Society

Northfield
The James Gang's Last Holdup
The good folk of Minnesota might seem like a slow-to-rile bunch, but
tell that to the James and Younger brothers. When these desperadoes

galloped into Northfield on September 7, 1876, they expected to ride back out with a few sacks full of cash . . . but that didn't happen.

The eight robbers that fateful day included Jesse and Frank James, Clell Miller, Big Bill Stiles (also known as Bill Chadwell), Charley Pitts (also known as George Wells), and Cole, James, and Bob Younger. Things started going wrong from the beginning for the outlaws. Local citizen J. S. Allen saw three unknown men with full-length, gun-hiding linen dusters heading into the bank, and was stopped from snooping by a fourth. He ran off down Division Street screaming, "Get your guns, boys—they're robbing the bank!" And the folks of Northfield *did* get their guns. *Lots* of guns.

Meanwhile, the robbers inside the bank were demanding that employee Joseph Lee Heywood open the safe. Heywood claimed it had a Yale chronometer lock, which was true, but he failed to mention that the timer had not been set—the door was actually unlocked. His word was all that kept the robbers from checking. For his supposed honesty, Heywood was pistol-whipped. Outside, the rest of the gang was riding up and down the street ordering everyone off the sidewalks. Nicholas Gustavson, a Swedish immigrant who didn't understand their shouts, was gunned down.

The outlaw gang fared even worse. From rooftops and open windows, citizens unloaded their guns at the bank robbers. Miller and Styles were shot dead, as was Bob Younger's horse. The three inside the bank grabbed about $15 that was sitting out and ran into the street. Before he left, Frank James shot and killed Heywood.

The six remaining outlaws rode southwest out of Northfield. (Pick up their story on page 140.) Charlie Pitts's body was taken on ice to St. Paul and displayed in the State Capitol for two days. A local doctor eventually retrieved the body and boiled it down for its skeleton. Clell Miller's corpse was scalped and its skeleton was eventually donated to the current museum dedicated to the shoot-out. The museum is housed in the old bank, and the teller cages and vault are exactly as they were during the robbery. Here you'll also see guns used by Cole Younger, Charlie Pitts, and Clell Miller during the shoot-out, and a pocket watch given to Dr. Henry Wheeler for gunning down Miller. Sadly, Miller's skeleton has been taken off display, though it is still in the museum's possession.

Northfield Historical Society, Scriver Building, 408 Division St., Northfield, MN 55057

(800) 658-2548 or (507) 645-9268

Hours: June–August, Monday–Wednesday, Friday–Saturday, 10 A.M.–4 P.M., Thursday 10 A.M.–8 P.M., Sunday 1–4 P.M.; September–May, Tuesday–Saturday, 10 A.M.–4 P.M., Sunday 1–4 P.M.

Cost: Adults $2, Kids (13 and under) $1.50

www.northfieldhistory.org or www.northfieldchamber.com

Directions: Between 4th and 5th Sts. on Rte. 246 (Division St.), just east of the river.

Northfield celebrates Defeat of Jesse James Days every year on the weekend after Labor Day. Over the course of the weekend, locals reenact the shoot-out six times.

Defeat of Jesse James Days, PO Box 23, Northfield, MN 55057

www.defeatofjessejamesdays.org

THE CIVIL WAR MADE 'EM DO IT?

Some folks say the Northfield raid was the last battle of the Civil War, especially considering the outcome. Most of the outlaws, including the Jameses and the Youngers, were former Confederate guerrillas with Quantrill's raiders. The First National Bank, on the other hand, had two former Union generals, Benjamin Butler and Adelbert Ames, as primary depositors. Ames, the carpetbagger governor of Mississippi, was so infamous in the South that his face was printed inside chamber pots.

Once again, the North whipped the South's butt. When the Younger family years later petitioned the Minnesota governor for a pardon, they used the excuse that the Civil War had turned the boys to a life of crime, and this somehow cleared them of full responsibility.

WABASHA

Wabasha celebrates Grumpy Old Men Days in late February each year. The 1993 movie was set in Wabasha, but mostly filmed in Faribault. The bar where **Jack Lemmon** and **Walter Matthau** hang out, Slippery's (10 Church St., www.slipperys.nv.switchboard.com), named for a 40-pound catfish, runs the movie nonstop.

Do not try this at home.

Owatonna
Casey Jones's Locomotive and the P-38s

The Heritage Halls Transportation and Children's Museum seems to have violated the first rule of museum fundraising: make 'em pay to see your best stuff. Though there are plenty of nifty displays inside this museum (old planes, cars, and farm equipment), the two most impressive items are outside . . . in the parking lot!

The first is Old Number 201, a train reportedly once engineered by Casey Jones. Unlike his final locomotive, he didn't blow this one up.

The other outdoor item is a massive sculpture of three P-38 fighter jets, each mounted on an arching pedestal. According to the museum, this sculpture can withstand winds of up to 100 MPH, which is the least you would expect from supersonic planes.

Heritage Halls Transportation & Children's Museum, 2300 Heritage Pl., Owatonna,
MN 55060

(888) 317-0057 or (507) 451-2060

Hours: September–May, Monday–Friday 9 A.M.–5 P.M., Saturday–Sunday 10 A.M.–5 P.M.;
June–August, Monday–Friday 9 A.M.–6 P.M., Saturday–Sunday 10 A.M.–6 P.M.

Cost: Adults $6, Seniors $5.50, Kids (2–12) $4

www.heritagehalls.org

Directions: Exit 45 from I-35, on the west side of the highway.

The Jewel Box

If your family jewels are particularly large, and you're looking for a safe place to put them, perhaps you should consider bringing them to the Wells Fargo Bank in Owatonna: the Jewel Box. This 1908 structure was designed by architect Louis Sullivan and is his best-known bank. The cubical building has high, arched, stained-glass windows inlaid with gold leaf; green exterior ornaments (some claim there are more than 200 color shades); and two-ton electric chandeliers to illuminate the interior murals.

The Jewel Box has changed ownership over the years, but has always remained a bank. It was featured on a U.S. postage stamp in 1981, and in 1997 it underwent extensive restoration. Visitors are welcome during regular banking hours.

Wells Fargo Bank (former National Farmers Bank), 101 N. Cedar St., Owatonna,
MN 55060

(507) 451-5670

Hours: Monday–Friday 9 A.M.–5 P.M.

Cost: Free

Directions: Downtown, on the north side of the square, at Broadway.

Owatonna and East Grand Forks
Cabela's Outfitters

Cabela's isn't a place for animal lovers unless, in addition to loving them, you'd like to hook, snare, trap, or shoot them as well. Filled with stuffed wildlife in dynamic poses, Cabela's retail outlets are kind of like natural history museums . . . but with ammo. There are seven stores around the upper Midwest; two of them are in Minnesota.

The larger of the two is located on the northwest side of Owatonna. You'll enter past two jumping whitetail deer, surrounded by a semicircle of a dozen mounted stag heads. At the back wall is Cabela's signature mountain of critters, a fake rock outcropping covered in regional huntable wildlife. In the fishing section you'll see more active wildlife in their enormous freshwater tank—just imagine yourself reeling in one of these babies! Now go and buy a new reel!

3900 Cabela Dr., Owatonna, MN 55060

(800) 581-4420 or (507) 451-4545

Hours: Monday–Saturday 8 A.M.–9 P.M., Sunday 10 A.M.–6 P.M.

Cost: Free

www.cabelas.com

Directions: Exit 45 from I-35, on the west side of the highway.

Cabela's northernmost retail outlet also has another freshwater tank. The store takes a Great White North approach to the species it has chosen for the critter mountain. Two moose bulls lock racks in battle. Wolves prowl in search of prey. And two majestic polar bears dominate the scene. One stands on its hind legs as if to say, "Welcome folks! Glad to see ya!" Of course, that was probably not the final sentiment to go through his head.

210 DeMers Ave. NW, East Grand Forks, MN 56721

(800) 581-4420 or (218) 773-0282

Hours: Monday–Saturday 8 A.M.–9 P.M., Sunday 10 A.M.–6 P.M.

Cost: Free

www.cabelas.com

Directions: Just east of the river on Rte. 287 (DeMers Ave.).

Preston, Wykoff, and Taylors Falls
Nights in Jail

Even if you don't have some sort of court order demanding that you spend an evening in the clink, there are a few jails in Minnesota where you're welcomed with open arms . . . and they give you the keys to escape! No fewer than *three* small towns have converted their old pokeys into charming B&Bs.

By far the largest and most elaborate is the Jail House Inn in Preston. The former Fillmore County Jail, constructed in 1869, has a dozen suites, but not all of them are for people with *Oz* fetishes. Only one of the rooms has its original bars, the Cell Block, with two queen-size beds. There are several other rooms with law enforcement themes: the Detention Room, the Court Room, the Drunk Tank, and the Processing Room. No need to worry about shower fights, but there is a communal double whirlpool. If you're coming for a conjugal visit, try the Bridal Suite.

Jail House Inn, 109 Houston St. NW, PO Box 422, Preston, MN 55965

(507) 765-2181

E-mail: sbinjail@rconnect.com

Hours: Check-in 3–6 P.M., Check-out 11 A.M.

Cost: $49–$189/night, depending on day and room

www.jailhouseinn.com

Directions: Between Preston and Fillmore Sts. on Houston St., one block west of St. Paul St. (Rte. 17).

Your room options at the Wykoff Jail Haus are limited, as there's only one cell with two bunks. This puny prison was constructed in 1913 and claims to be the smallest B&B in Minnesota. There's not even room in this shoebox of a building for an on-site manager, so you don't have to worry about some little old lady or bad-ass sheriff banging on the bars and interrupting your incarceration.

Wykoff Jail Haus, Front & Main Sts., PO Box 205, Wykoff, MN 55990

(507) 352-4205

Hours: Incarceration (check-in) 3–6 P.M., Parole (check-out) Noon

Cost: $58/queen bed; $13.50/bunk bed

www.dwave.net/~schnabl/WykoffMN.htm#attractions

Directions: Just north of Rte. 80 (Front St.) on Main St.

Another little lockup, this one built in 1884, can be found a little farther north along the Mississippi River in Taylors Falls. The Old Jail Bed & Breakfast was constructed using a method called cribbing, in which two-by-fours are sandwiched together to make the walls. It isn't exactly escape-proof, but as crazy as this B&B is, who'd want to? There are three suites at the Old Jail, and each has its own entrance. You won't be processed with a bunch of strangers. Inmates who want a breakfast must make their own using the in-room kitchen facilities—this is not a place that believes in coddling its guests.

Old Jail Bed & Breakfast, 349 Government St., PO Box 203, Taylors Falls, MN 55084

(651) 465-3112

E-mail: oldjail@scc.net

Hours: Call for availability

Cost: $110–$130

www.oldjail.com

Directions: One block west of Rte. 8 where it turns to the Mississippi River bridge.

Rochester
Doc Graham's Grave

Doctor Archibald Graham played a minor but significant part in the 1989 movie *Field of Dreams*, and though the film is pure fiction, Graham was not. "Moonlight" Graham played one inning for the New York Giants on June 29, 1905, and never got to bat. When told he would be sent to the minors after the shortest major-league career in history, he opted to return to the University of Maryland to finish his medical degree. After interning in New York City, he showed up at the Rood Hospital in Chisholm, Minnesota, in 1909, where he would work for eight years. From there, he became the doctor for the Chisholm school district, where he served another 44 years. Everyone agreed that he was one of the nicest guys in town. He retired in 1961, died in 1965, and was buried in downstate Rochester.

He might have been forgotten had not writers W. P. Kinsella and J. D. Salinger come to town in 1977 and started asking a lot of questions. Kinsella incorporated Graham into his book *Shoeless Joe*, which was later made into the film *Field of Dreams*. Burt Lancaster played the aging Doc Graham. (The reclusive Salinger was fictionalized as Terence Mann in the film, played by James Earl Jones.) In the book and movie, "Moonlight" (nicknamed because of his insomnia) comes back to life to get his first and only at-bat against a field of all-stars, then gives it up to rescue a girl choking on a hot dog. It's more touching than it sounds.

Don't believe all you see in pictures—Graham does not walk the streets of Chisholm as a ghost. He's quite dead, and you can still find him in Rochester.

Calvary Cemetery, 2706 Fourth Ave. NW, Rochester, MN 55901

(507) 289-0183

Hours: Daylight hours

Cost: Free

Directions: East of Rte. 52 (18th Ave.) on Eaton Hills Dr., turn north on 4th Ave.; Section 9, Lot 4, Plot 1E.

Electroshock and Presidential Surgery

The Mayo Clinic has long been a center of top-notch medical care and groundbreaking therapies. The clinic has an impressive list of successfully treated patients, some of them famous, but there are also a few less-than-successful stories.

Take the case of Ernest Hemingway. He commuted to the clinic from his Idaho home in 1960 to receive electroshock therapy for depression. The treatments apparently didn't work, for after returning to the spud state he blew his brains out in what some tried to call a "gun cleaning accident."

Another patient, Korean War veteran Thomas Eagleton, received electroshock treatment to help him overcome combat stress after returning stateside. It seemed to work, but that didn't matter in 1972. By then he was a senator and a virtual shoe-in for the Democratic vice-presidential nomination with George McGovern. When it was revealed that Eagleton had taken a little juice between the ears, party faithfuls urged that his nomination go instead to Sargent Shriver, and it did.

The Mayo Clinic was also where Ronald Reagan had brain surgery at the end of his second term in 1988. What, if anything, they found in his skull is still protected by patient confidentiality. George Bush, Sr., had a hip replaced at the clinic on December 5, 2000.

The clinic once had a nifty museum with such informative displays as the Farm Accident exhibit where you could find a 3-D cutaway of a rectum and bladder impaled on a pitchfork—ouch!—but now you must settle for a tour of the facilities.

Mayo Clinic, 200 First St. SW, Rochester, MN 55905

(507) 284-2450

Tour Hours: Monday–Friday 10 A.M.

Cost: Free

Directions: Two blocks west of Rte. 63 (Broadway), one block south of Center St.

Ear-normous.

World's Largest Ear of Corn

While this guidebook has demonstrated that Minnesotans aren't afraid to be goofy, deep down they are a practical bunch, and sometimes their no-nonsense cores can influence their nonsensical activities. Take the World's Largest Ear of Corn, a massive cob that juts skyward from a food plant on the south side of Rochester. The 60-foot ear on a 150-foot pedestal is illuminated at night by a half-dozen floodlights to prevent anyone from forgetting the town's corny superiority after sunset.

But this mighty vegetable is more than a source of civic pride—it's also a working water tower for the Seneca Foods Plant, which is affiliated with Libby's. Corn products pay the bills around here, and the owners wanted to return the favor.

Libby's Seneca Foods Plant, 1217 3rd Ave. SE, Rochester, MN 55904

(507) 280-4500

Hours: Always visible

Cost: Free

www.rochestercvb.org

Directions: Two blocks east of Broadway (Rte. 63), on 12th St. SE.

Rollingstone
The Minnesota Iceman

In 1968, retired air force pilot and Minnesota farmer Frank Hansen started touring county fairs and shopping malls with what *he* called the Siberskoye Creature, but which is more often referred to as the Minnesota Iceman. This half-man, half-ape creature was entombed in a 3,000-pound block of hazy ice. The specimen was about six feet tall, had large hands, was hairy, and was reportedly well-endowed. The Iceman had apparently been shot in his right eye, which was hanging out of its socket, and had the back of his head blown out. Who killed it? Nobody would fess up; all that was said was that it had been found in the Sea of Okhotsk by Russian seal hunters.

Was it the Abominable Snowman? (Wilder stories say it was a Tok, a southeast Asian Yeti, that was accidentally killed during the Vietnam War, then smuggled into the United States by the CIA in a body bag.) Its owner, an unnamed California millionaire, had hired Hansen to tour the country for two years with one restriction: never unfreeze the body for examination. Apparently, the owner didn't want to upset humankind's notions of creation. At least not too much.

However, two cryptozoologists, Dr. Bernard Heuvelmans (from Belgium's Royal Institute of Natural Sciences) and Dr. Ivan Sanderson (science editor of *Argosy* magazine), examined it through the ice at Hansen's Pipestone farm and proclaimed it a genuine "living fossil"—whatever that is. Heuvelmans sprang this big news on Johnny Carson's *Tonight Show* in December 1968.

Shortly thereafter, they detailed their findings in an *Argosy* magazine article. They dubbed the creature Bozo, gave it a Latin classification of *Homo pongides*, and openly suggested that they'd identified a Neanderthal, or perhaps Darwin's missing link. Their reasoning was clouded by their egos, as detailed in their summary: "You can't completely fool two trained morphologists with zoological, anatomical, and anthropological training. No! Bozo is the genuine article." The Smithsonian was now apparently very interested in purchasing it. The museum persuaded border officials to stop Hansen from bringing the touring Iceman back into the United States at the Canadian border and would have seized the specimen had not then-senator Walter Mondale intervened on Hansen's behalf.

But Heuvelmans and Sanderson turned out to be the Bozos when word got out that the Minnesota Iceman was built by Disney model-maker Howard Ball. Some came to the scientists' defense and claimed that the current Minnesota Iceman was a replica of the original, which is now back with its California benefactor.

Private Address, Rollingstone, MN 55969
Private phone
Hours: Private property; view from road
Cost: Free
www.n2.net/prey/bigfoot/articles/argosy2.htm
Directions: Ask around town, if you dare.

WINONA

Winona Ryder's parents displayed a shocking lack of creativity when they named their daughter after her birthplace on October 29, 1971. Her birth name is Winona Horowitz, and her godfather was **Timothy Leary**.

Winona's first name was Montezuma. It was renamed to honor an Indian woman who threw herself from nearby Maiden Rock.

Stephen Taylor, buried in Winona, is the only Revolutionary soldier buried in the state.

Not Bud's best ad.

Spring Grove
Belly by Budweiser

Boy, you just can't get good advertising like the kind you'll see in Spring Grove. Just north of the town square is a concrete statue of a human-size troll waving an Uf-Da flag. He clearly couldn't be pregnant, but yet he appears to be so.

Ahhhh, the sign says it all: "Belly by Budweiser." Obviously this statue was made before the era of Bud Lite.

Maple Dr. & 1st Ave. NE, Spring Grove, MN 55974

No phone

Hours: Always visible

Cost: Free

www.springgrovemn.com

Directions: On the north side of the town park on Rte. 44 (Main St.).

Wabasha
Arrowhead Bluffs Exhibit

Les and John Behrns like to shoot things, and the proof is in this museum. Virtually every animal in this private museum was felled by one or the other of these guys, from the largest moose to the smallest squirrel. Currently more than 70 stuffed critters are mounted throughout the building, but there's room for many more.

The Arrowhead Bluffs Exhibit also contains at least one model of every Winchester firearm ever made; it's the only place in the world where they can all be seen at one time. In addition, there are dioramas of a meat-processing operation, model trains, Native American artifacts, and lots of old photographs.

RR 2, PO Box 7, Wabasha, MN 55981

(651) 565-3829

Hours: May–December, daily 10 A.M.–6 P.M.

Cost: Adults $4, Teens (12–18) $3, Kids (6–11) $2

Directions: On Rte. 60, south of town, at the top of the bluffs.

Cathouse B&B

Friends and coworkers might look at you funny if you tell them you're going to spend the night in a cathouse . . . with your family. But the 1856 Anderson House B&B isn't some sort of Minnesota brothel; it's the oldest operating motel west of the Mississippi. They just happen to pimp a dozen mighty fine cats.

They call them Sleeper Cats, and when you make a reservation, be sure to sign one up to keep your feet warm. Each cat is delivered to your room with a litter box, bowls of food and water, and a set of operating instructions. The kitties go fast, so book your sleeper in advance. And if you're not really a cat person, you can always request a heated brick to put at the foot of the bed—the front desk will deliver one in a quilted sleeve to warm your cold, cold, cat-hating heart.

Anderson House, 333 W. Main St., Wabasha, MN 55981

(800) 535-5467 or (651) 565-4524

Hours: Open year-round

Cost: $89–$154/night; sleeper cats, no charge

www.theandersonhouse.com

Directions: One block from the river, two blocks north of the bridge.

Wabasha's Smithsonian.

Suilmann's Grotto and Museum

While the notion that a man's home is his castle seems a little outdated, the idea that his garage is his museum is downright weird. Unless that man is Joe Suilmann. This retiree has turned a carport into a museum of anything and everything he finds interesting. Small carvings of Abraham Lincoln, bottles of sand from around the world, howitzer shells, food tins, rusty guns, fishing lures . . . and that's just on one shelf. Even a few neighborhood dogs and cats have been preserved for the ages through the miracle of taxidermy.

Outside in the yard are concrete replicas of forts, churches, and other buildings—Suilmann's Grotto. Joe will give you the personal tour, pointing out each item and asking "Did ya ever see anything like that before?" And chances are you haven't, unless you've rooted around your grandparents' attic. But once you're done here, your worldview will be expanded considerably.

118 Hiawatha Dr. E., Wabasha, MN 55981

Private phone

Hours: Hours vary

Cost: Adults 25¢

Directions: At Bailey Ave. and Hiawatha Dr., one block east of Pembroke Ave. (Rte. 60).

Winona
Dead Priests

Father Lawrence Lesches was insane. He did not take it well when Bishop Heffron, president of St. Mary's College, told him he was better cut out to be a farmer . . . away from humans. So Lesches shot the bishop, three times, while he was standing at the altar conducting mass.

Lesches turned out to be no better a shot than he was a priest; the bishop survived to see Lesches locked up in the State Hospital for the Dangerously Insane in St. Peter. After the priest spent a few years wrapped in wet sheets, the hospital staff thought he'd made tremendous progress and recommended that he be released. But the bishop would have none of that, and Lesches remained locked up and eventually died there. He was buried in the college cemetery, but he did not rest in peace.

Odd things began to happen at St. Mary's. One campus priest died in a fire. Three more priests were killed in an airplane crash. And in a bizarre electrocution, Father Lynch (a friend of the bishop) fried himself, a Bible in one hand a lamp cord in the other. His charred body was found lying perpendicular across a bed forming a blackened human crucifix.

Not long thereafter work was completed on Heffron Hall, named after the retiring president . . . who would soon die of cancer. This dormitory seems to have focused all of the dead priest's psychic energy. Students have spotted the ghost of Father Lesches wandering the frigid halls.

Heffron Hall, St. Mary's College, 700 Terrace Heights, Winona, MN 55987

(507) 452-4430

Hours: Always visible; campus is private

Cost: Free

Directions: South two blocks on Rte. 14 from Rte. 61, turn left onto campus, follow the road left.

Wykoff
Ed's Museum

When Edwin Kruger's wife Lydia died in 1940, the only person who was ever able to keep his hoarding habit in check was gone. Kruger had opened a Jack Sprat store in Wykoff in 1933, and he was the kind of merchant every small town needs: the guy who has everything. Oh, whatever the Wykoff folks needed might have been a little dusty, but it was better than driving all the way to Rochester.

Upon Kruger's death in 1989, the store was willed to the town. The women of the Wykoff Progress Club pulled out their sponges and pails, rolled up their sleeves, and set to scrubbing the Jack Sprat. To their credit, they didn't try to erase the memory of the packrat neighbor they loved so dearly—they just wanted to tidy things up. Said one volunteer, "We don't try to understand it—we just organized it."

Fair enough. And what did they find? *TV Guides* from 1954 to 1989. Boxes filled with scraps of string. Candy from the 1930s, gnawed by mice. A baby food jar containing the 25 gallstones Ed passed during his lifetime. Another jar with his kid's baby teeth, unclaimed by the Tooth Fairy. New clothing in unopened boxes, gifts to Ed from the Wykoff Progress Club (who always felt frumpy Ed, bless his heart, needed a makeover).

And the artifact visitors most want to see? Sammy the Cat. Ed's feline companion went to that great scratching post in the sky in 1986, so Kruger laid his earthly vessel in a shoebox, which he then placed on a basement shelf. Sammy's still there.

Jack Sprat Food Store, 100 S. Gold St., Wykoff, MN 55990

(507) 352-4205

Hours: June–September, Saturday–Sunday 1–4 P.M., or by appointment

Cost: $2 donation

Directions: On Rte. 80 (Gold St.) north of Pearl St.

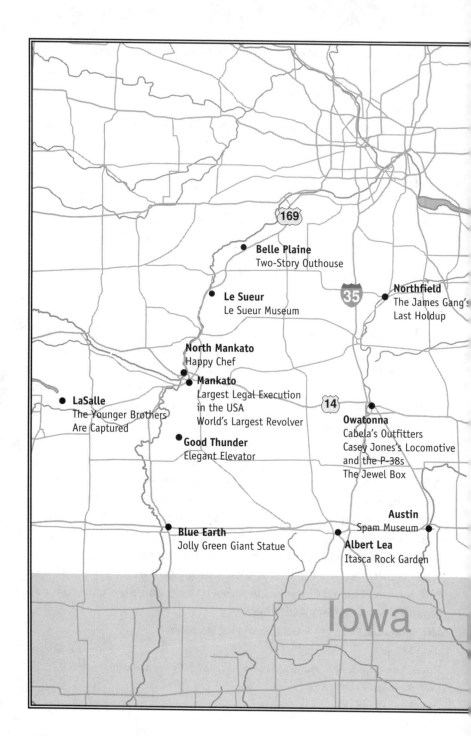

Belle Plaine
Two-Story Outhouse

169

35

Northfield
The James Gang's
Last Holdup

Le Sueur
Le Sueur Museum

North Mankato
Happy Chef

Mankato
Largest Legal Execution
in the USA
World's Largest Revolver

14

LaSalle
The Younger Brothers
Are Captured

Owatonna
Cabela's Outfitters
Casey Jones's Locomotive
and the P-38s
The Jewel Box

Good Thunder
Elegant Elevator

Austin
Spam Museum

Blue Earth
Jolly Green Giant Statue

Albert Lea
Itasca Rock Garden

Iowa

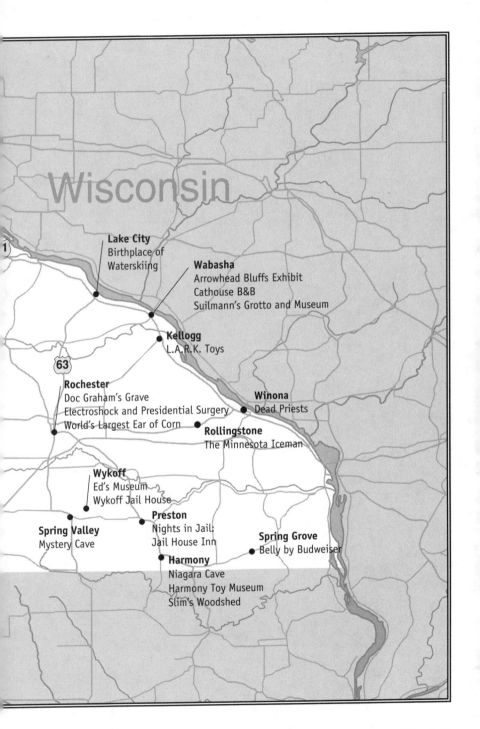

Wisconsin

Lake City
Birthplace of
Waterskiing

Wabasha
Arrowhead Bluffs Exhibit
Cathouse B&B
Suilmann's Grotto and Museum

Kellogg
L.A.R.K. Toys

63

Rochester
Doc Graham's Grave
Electroshock and Presidential Surgery
World's Largest Ear of Corn

Winona
Dead Priests

Rollingstone
The Minnesota Iceman

Wykoff
Ed's Museum
Wykoff Jail House

Preston
Nights in Jail:
Jail House Inn

Spring Valley
Mystery Cave

Spring Grove
Belly by Budweiser

Harmony
Niagara Cave
Harmony Toy Museum
Slim's Woodshed

5

THE TWIN CITIES

*T*hough they are called the Twin Cities, Minneapolis and St. Paul are far from identical. Garrison Keillor once observed, "The difference between St. Paul and Minneapolis is the difference between pumpernickel and Wonder Bread." There is more than a little bias toward pumpernickel in that assessment, which you might expect from a St. Paul booster. But it's only fair to note that some people like Wonder Bread.

To get a sense of which town you might like best, scan the history books and compare who and what these two cities have contributed to the world. James Arness, Peter Graves, Prince, Jesse "The Body/Mind" Ventura, Richard Dean Anderson, Mike Todd, J. Paul Getty, and Terry Gilliam were all born in Minneapolis. St. Paul gave us Loni Anderson, LeRoy Neiman, F. Scott Fitzgerald, Supreme Court Chief Justice Warren Burger, DeWitt Wallace (founder of *Reader's Digest*), and William Demarest, as well as the first grocery bag with handles and the home water softener. Point St. Paul.

What about quality of life? Minneapolis prides itself on being more progressive and orderly than St. Paul. While St. Paul has antiquated driving laws, like the one demanding that if you come across a horse-drawn carriage you must stop, get out, and help the horse pass. In Minneapolis, however, a judge may, by law, sentence a double-parker to a chain gang. Point Minneapolis.

St. Paul citizens turn their noses up at their twin as "Minnie No-Place" or "Minnie-Hopeless," while Minneapolis residents dismiss their eastern neighbor as "St. Small."

The debate goes on and on. You're better off deciding for yourself. The vacation destinations in this chapter ought to help.

Minneapolis
Action Squad!

So you want to get to know the Twin Cities? Why not start from the inside and work out? And by inside, I mean *inside*. Back in 1996, a group of students from the University of Minnesota at Minneapolis formed Action Squad to explore the campus's steam tunnels. After succeeding (and more easily than they expected!) they started branching out to the rest of the city. The Cambridge Mental Hospital tunnels. The Fort Snelling drains. The Ford Motors mines. The Temple of the Drowned Cat. They were hooked.

Some might dismiss the Action Squad as a bunch of trespassing hooligans, but they'd be wrong. The group has a strict code of conduct that sounds suspiciously like Star Trek's Prime Directive: no theft, return things to their original condition, no vandalism, and no D.W.A.S. (Drinking While Action Squadding). They aim to keep their group elite because they fear if knowledge of how to access the off-limits sites became widely available, the city's sewers would be overrun by drunken frat boys and gang taggers. Still, they just can't keep their fantastic adventures to themselves—and why should they?

That's where Action Squad's Web site comes in handy. The site's disclaimer states " . . . it should serve as a safe and societally acceptable means for people to experience activities of a dangerous and legally questionable nature from the comfort and safety of their homes." And how! On it you'll find hundreds of Action Squad photos of members slogging through storm drains, rapelling into brewery caves, and posing on abandoned machinery from the cities' infrastructure—always with their eyes blocked out with tabloidesque black boxes. Totally cool.

The Bat Cave, Minneapolis, MN 55414
No phone
Hours: Always visible . . . on the Web
Cost: Free
www.actionsquad.org
Directions: They won't tell you.

MINNEAPOLIS
Eighteen workers were killed in Minneapolis when the Washburn "A" flour mill exploded on May 2, 1878.

The Bakken: A Museum and Library of Electricity in Life

At last, a museum that lives up to its grandiose title! The Bakken began as the private collection of Earl Bakken, the inventor of the wearable cardiac pacemaker and later founder of Medtronic. He must have made scads of money, because his company ponied up the dough for this one-of-a-kind museum on the many uses of electricity and magnetism in medicine (and elsewhere).

They've got Benjamin Franklin's writings on electricity, and his glass harmonica; they've got Duchenne's medical coil for faradic stimulation; they've got Tesla's D'Arsonval Spiral, a cure-all electric field generator; and they've got the original research notes of Allesandro Volta and Luigi Galvani. They've even got aquariums, called Electrariums, filled with electric eels. These critters were once thought to have curative powers, if only you'd grab them. (Don't try it here; the docents will get upset.) And did you know Alexander Graham Bell used an early metal detector to find the bullet lodged in President Garfield? Simply shocking!

In all, the Bakken has more than 2,000 artifacts and 12,000 books for you to enjoy. The museum prides itself on injecting a sense of fun into its displays. In one, you'll see a video of a frog levitated using a magnetic field that is 100,000 times as strong as the Earth's. In another, you'll see scientist August Waller testing out his new invention, the 1887 electrocardiograph machine, on his pet bulldog Jim. To read the dog's heart rate, the poor pooch had to stand patiently in two basins of salt water. Finally, the museum's newest exhibit is a multimedia presentation of Mary Shelley's *Frankenstein*. Watch as a lifeless creature comes to life in the scientist's laboratory, and hear the story of how it came to a tragic end. Clearly, not all electricity is used for a higher purpose!

3537 Zenith Ave. S, Minneapolis, MN 55416

(612) 927-6508

Hours: Tuesday–Saturday 10 A.M.–5 P.M.; Library Monday–Friday 9 A.M.–4:30 P.M.

Cost: Adults $5, Seniors $3, Kids $3

www.thebakken.org

Directions: South on W. Calhoun Pkwy. From Lake St. (Rte. 3), on the western shore of Lake Calhoun.

Cunanan's Spree Begins

It was the crime spree that gripped the nation (or at least the news media) in the summer of 1997. Andrew Cunanan left a trail of death and destruction across the United States, and it all started in Minneapolis.

What drove Cunanan to murder Jeffrey Trail in the Harmony Lofts on April 27, 1997, isn't entirely known since all who were there that night died before revealing the story. Cunanan had arrived in town from San Diego two days earlier and spent the first night with architect David Madson in the trendy Warehouse District. The following night he was at Trail's apartment. Trail knew Cunanan from San Diego; he was out of town for the weekend.

When Trail returned Sunday night, he stopped by Madson's to see Cunanan before he was to leave town the next day. While Madson was out walking his dog, Cunanan snapped (again, there are many theories, ranging from spurned advances to a steroid-induced rage) and he beat Trail to death with a claw hammer. Madson returned to find Trail's body wrapped up in a floor rug, and Cunanan with a gun.

Contrary to earlier reports of collusion, it appears Madson was held against his will in the apartment. Cunanan went with Madson to walk his Dalmatian, Prints (today, the dog formerly known as Prints), all the while with a gun hidden under his long coat. The pair left town in Madson's jeep two days later.

Harmony Lofts, Apt. 404, 240 2nd Ave. N, Minneapolis, MN 55401
No phone
Hours: Always visible
Cost: Free
Directions: On the corner of 2nd Ave. N and Washington Ave. N.

Cunanan and Madson drove north on I-35 from the Twin Cities. Cunanan probably promised Madsen he would release him far from the city, giving Cunanan time to make a getaway before Madson could find a phone. Madson got out of the jeep, or was ordered out, near an abandoned farmhouse on East Rush Lake, and then Cunanan shot him three times. (Reports that the pair was seen scarfing down cheeseburgers and having a few beers at the Full Moon Bar in nearby Stark were wrong—the coroner found no food in Madson's stomach during the autopsy.)

Madson's body was not found until the following Saturday. By then, Trail's body had already been discovered, as had that of Cunanan's next victim, Lee Miglin, in Chicago.

East Rush Lake, Stark, MN 55032

No phone

Hours: Always visible

Cost: Free

Directions: A half mile south of the boat landing on the northeast corner of East Rush Lake.

Dillon . . . No, No . . . Dylan

Before he took the stage in 1960 for the first time, young Robert Zimmerman told the manager of the Ten O'Clock Scholar (416 14th Avenue SE) that his stage name was Bob Dillon. When later asked why, he claimed it was an homage to Dylan Thomas. Upon being informed of the correct spelling of the name of the poet he so deeply admired, he changed it to the name he goes by today.

You can hardly blame the guy for being confused, having recently arrived from Hibbing to attend the University of Minnesota. He landed at Sigma Alpha Mu (925 University Avenue SE), the school's Jewish fraternity, in a neighborhood known as Dinkeytown. He didn't quite fit in with the frat house scene, and moved out a few months later into an apartment above Gray's Drug Store.

There's precious little left for Dylan fans to see in the Twin Cities today. Both the Ten O'Clock Scholar and Sigma Alpha Mu have been torn down. But Dylan's former apartment still exists. In fact, you can still rent his old room.

329 14th Ave. SE, Minneapolis, MN 55414

Private phone

Hours: Always visible

Cost: Free

Directions: Between University Ave. and 4th St. SE on 14th Ave.

MINNEAPOLIS
If you rub the big toe on the statue *Mississippi, Father of Waters* in the Minneapolis City Hall (5th St. and 3rd Avenue S), it is supposed to bring you good luck.

Foshay Tower

Opened on August 30, 1929, on the eve of the Great Depression, the Foshay Tower was designed with the Washington Monument as its driving inspiration. In fact, the design appears to be a fatter, windowed, Art Deco version of the monument. Financier Wilbur Foshay had seen the obelisk as a teenager and vowed to build his own if he ever got the money.

So, later in life when he found himself rolling in dough from his successful Midwest utility endeavors, he had somebody design his dreamscraper. Construction began in 1927. It was the first skyscraper in Minneapolis, soaring 447 feet above the street. Foshay asked that it have a super-cool penthouse suite on the 32nd floor—his suite—and it was here that he had the building's inaugural banquet. The party was a grand affair. It even had its own theme song, "Foshay Tower—A Washington Memorial," penned by guest of honor John Philip Sousa.

But before Foshay paid the $116,449 bill for the bash, Black Thursday wiped out his finances. The party was never paid for, and Sousa's check bounced. Foshay went to Leavenworth for mail fraud in 1932.

Today the tower stands in a forest of skyscrapers that hide its long-ago status as the tallest building west of the Mississippi (and the tallest building in Minneapolis until 1971). A museum of Foshayabilia is located on the 31st floor, surrounded by an open-air observation deck.

821 Marquette Ave. S, Minneapolis, MN 55402

(612) 359-3030

Hours: Monday–Friday Noon–4 P.M., Saturday 11 A.M.–3 P.M.

Cost: Adults $4, Seniors $2, Kids $2

Directions: One block east of the Nicollet Mall at Marquette St. and S. 9th St.

MINNEAPOLIS LAWS

★ Driving a car while using snuff is against the law.

★ Male dancers must wear a cravat somewhere on their person.

★ You may not keep a goat in your apartment, but you can have a mule.

★ If you replace a bathtub, it must have legs.

Tams are all around, no need to waste them . . .
Photo by Jim Frost

Mary Richards's Home Turf

Sure, Minneapolis existed before 1970 when Mary Richards came to town, but who knew? Certainly not a lot of American television viewers. But when that spunky single gal tossed her hat into the air at the end of the *Mary Tyler Moore Show's* opening credits, the nation sat up in its collective La-Z-Boy. Over its seven-year run, the sitcom held a commanding position atop the Nielsen ratings and garnered 29 Emmys.

When the show premiered, Mary moved into a funky studio apartment with a sunken living room and a foldout bed. Her kooky new landlord, Phyllis, had promised the apartment to Rhoda, a cynical New Yorker who was living in the converted attic. Despite the initial tension between Mary and Rhoda, the pair became fast friends during the first 30-minute episode. Mary hung her big M on her wall, and called it home. She also landed a job as the assistant producer at WJM the same day—that woman was a dynamo! Though her address was said to be 119 N. Weatherly (Apartment D), the exterior shot was of a home in Minneapolis's Kenwood Park neighborhood, just west of where she fed the ducks in Loring Park.

First Apartment Site, 2104 Kenwood Parkway, Minneapolis, MN 55405
Private phone
Hours: Always visible; view from street
Cost: Free
www.mtmshow.com
Directions: On the southwest corner, at 21st St.

Four years later, after Phyllis had departed for San Francisco and Rhoda for New York, Mary was forced out of her apartment due to political unrest—not on the show, in real life. Apparently the owner of the Minneapolis home insisted on hanging an "Impeach Nixon" sign in Mary's window. Producers didn't want fans who came to the Twin Cities to think Mary Richards was some sort of crazy radical, so they moved her into a high-rise apartment near downtown.

Second Apartment Site, 7 Cedar Riverside Plaza, 1610 Sixth St. S, Minneapolis, MN 55454
Private phone
Hours: Always visible
Cost: Free
Directions: West of the UM campus, just east of the intersection of I-35W and I-94.

Sorry to break it to you MTM fans—the real Mary never spent much time in Minneapolis. She stepped inside her Kenwood Park apartment for the first time in 1996, on the invitation of the current owners. The opening credits were shot in the Twin Cities and the rest was filmed on a Hollywood sound stage.

As brief as the opening credits were, they made a couple places famous. The shot of her having lunch in the courtyard of the IDS Center was shot at Basil's Restaurant, where you can still ask for the Mary Table (Marquette Avenue and South 7th Street, (612) 376-7404). Be prepared to stand in a line behind other fans. It's just a short walk from the most famous MTM site in the city: the Hat Tossing Corner outside Marshall Field's. In 2002, TV Land paid for a $125,000 bronze statue of Mary to be placed on the Nicollet Mall, exactly where her enthusiasm for Minneapolis had got the better of her three decades earlier.

Hat Tossing Site, 700 Nicollet Pedestrian Mall, Minneapolis, MN 55402

No phone

Hours: Always visible

Cost: Free

Directions: At the corner of Nicollet and 7th Sts.

Minnesota Baseball Hall of Fame

There are few fans in the world like Ray Crump. This dedicated baseball lover has been with the Minnesota Twins since the days when they were the Washington Senators. He was 13 years old when he got a job as the club's bat boy. When the team moved to the Twin Cities, so did Crump. Through good times and bad, he's been there, and the result can be seen in the Minnesota Baseball Hall of Fame.

Crump's museum has everything you might expect in a collection dedicated to the Twins: baseballs, bats, jerseys, photos, and other souvenirs. But it also has plenty you'd never expect. Crump used his connections at venues around town to get backstage and meet every celebrity under the sun, and the photos on the walls prove it: hundreds, including Elvis, Liberace, Florence Henderson, Rip Taylor, and what appears to be the entire cast of *Hee Haw*. He's even got odd shots of the Beatles reclining on lumpy foldout beds before a concert. Most remarkable, however, is a collection of baseballs signed by folks who have very little to do with the sport—for example, Bob Hope, Milton Berle, and Mac Davis.

910 S. Third St., Minneapolis, MN 55415

(612) 375-9707

Hours: Monday–Friday 9 A.M.–4 P.M., Saturday 11 A.M.–3 P.M.; open later during game days

Cost: Free

Directions: Just northeast of the Hubert Humphrey Metrodome.

Cash cow for Sherwin Williams.

Polka Dot House

Long ago Mari Newman decided it wasn't worth her time to go looking for galleries to display her art—it was distracting her from actually making art. Instead, she figured the galleries would come to her if she put out the right advertisement. In 1989, with a few dozen gallons of house paint, she began daubing every color of the rainbow on the white siding of her Lake Harriet home. And then she painted her garage. And then her windows. And her stumps out front. And a shopping cart parked on the sidewalk. And the empty aluminum cans in the cart. You name it, she painted it, inside and outside, up and down.

Eventually, a few galleries did take notice, but by then Newman was only casually interested in their dealer-come-lately attention. Through sidewalk sales and drive-by visitors, she was already making enough money to buy art supplies and tobacco for her collection of pipes. The outside of her home is always changing, due in part to vandalism of misunderstood subjects she's chosen to portray. No matter—there's still more paint where the rest of it came from!

5117 Penn Ave. S, Minneapolis, MN 55419
Private phone
Hours: Always visible
Cost: Free
Directions: Just south of 51st St. on Penn Ave., due south of Lake Harriet.

Prince-0-Rama

No musician has made as big an impression on Minneapolis as the artist currently known as the artist formerly known as the Artist Formerly Known as Prince. Got it? No wonder he had to use that funky symbol!

It was all much easier to remember when he entered the world as Prince Rogers Nelson on June 7, 1958, at Mt. Sinai Hospital (2215 Park Avenue S). As a child growing up in Minneapolis, his family lived at 915 Logan Avenue, but he bounced around between his father's and mother's places after they divorced. Later he attended Central High (3416 3rd Avenue S) where he played on the basketball team and claimed his favorite class was "The Business of Music." Surprised?

Prince formed his first band, Grand Central, in his friend's basement. The group mostly played the hotel lounge circuit, much to the amusement of their friends. But nobody was laughing as that little guy in purple started making it big.

The most easily recognized Prince site in the Twin Cities is First Avenue (701 N. First Avenue N), a former Greyhound Station and the onetime focal point of the where-to-be-seen scene. Over the years, Prince played here 15 times. The club served as the location for 1984's *Purple Rain*, a movie loosely based on Prince's rise to funky stardom.

Prince took all the money he made on *Purple Rain* (which was a lot) and built one of the coolest studios around. You can pick it out in its otherwise boring office park by the purple pyramids on the roof. Not only does it look nifty on the outside, the inside has a history worth noting. Madonna, R.E.M., the Fine Young Cannibals, Paula Abdul, the Bodeans, and (of course) Prince have all recorded here. So have commercial musicians for Huggies diapers and Comet cleanser.

So what's Prince up to these days? Reportedly, he found God in 2001—and promptly said he would be going back to eliminate all the cuss words from his song lyrics.

Paisley Park Studios, 7801 Audubon Rd., Chanhassen, MN 55317
Private phone
Hours: Always visible
Cost: Free
Directions: At the intersection of Audubon Rd. and Arboretum Blvd.

MINNEAPOLIS

In front of a packed crowd at a traveling carnival in Minneapolis in 1872, Hermann the Hypnotist made Archie Collins fly up and out through the tent's roof, turned himself into a skeleton, levitated above the stage, and disappeared . . . forever. Neither Hermann nor Archie were ever found.

Poet **John Berryman** killed himself by jumping off the Washington Avenue Bridge in Minneapolis on January 7, 1972.

The fluorescent lighting in the Minneapolis Main Post Office (100 S. First Street) has been in continuous operation since 1925, the longest-running fluorescent lights in the nation.

In 1953, the U.S. army used Minneapolis neighborhoods to test zinc cadmium sulfide spray as a method of dispersing germs for warfare. Nobody in the neighborhoods was told about the tests.

Minnesota Vikingettes.

Sister Fun

Do you need a whoopee cushion, fast? How about a plastic hula skirt? Or a wind-up Japanese robot? Well, if you come to Sister Fun, you've found the right place. Owner Bobbette Axelrod has stuffed her store with plastic Viking helmets and Groucho glasses, fake doggie doo-doo and rubber rats, costume jewelry, and naughty refrigerator magnets—if it's tacky, goofy, tasteless, strange, silly, or odd, she's got it. Unless, of course, her tacky, goofy, tasteless, strange, silly, and odd customers have cleared her out. Then you'll have to settle for the wacky, gooey, bizarre, grotesque, and absurd.

You never know what you'll find each time you visit, which is part of the idea. Even if you don't have a pressing need for pink flamingo swizzle sticks or a mechanical man who blows bubbles from his behind, you may walk out having purchased it anyway. Think of it as an investment in your mental health. Trust me, you'll feel better for it.

1604 W. Lake, Minneapolis, MN 55408

(612) 672-0263

Hours: Tuesday–Saturday Noon–7 P.M., Sunday 1–5 P.M.

Cost: Free

Directions: Two blocks east of the Lake St./Lagoon Ave. merge at Calhoun Pkwy. East.

Longfellow wasn't here.

"The Song of Hiawatha" Waterfall

One of Henry Wadsworth Longfellow's best-known works, "The Song of Hiawatha," is a fictional Native American tale set in the upper Midwest using the name of an Iroquois chief who never came to this area. Supposedly Longfellow was inspired to write the poem after seeing the majestic 53-foot-tall Minnehaha Falls during a visit to Fort Snelling. That's partly true. He did see the falls, but most likely on a stereoscopic slide given to him by a soldier; he never made the hike over to the actual site.

Longfellow's poem was published in 1855, and became a classic with teachers, who forced their students to memorize it. Kids in Minnesota gathered their pennies to fund a statue of Hiawatha carrying his bride Minnehaha over the laughing waters. The life-sized bronze was designed by Jakob H. Fjelde and installed in 1912. It is dedicated to two people who never existed, who lived a story that never happened, written by a guy who never visited the place.

Minnehaha Park, 48th St. & Minnehaha Pkwy., Minneapolis, MN 55417

(612) 661-4806

Hours: Always visible

Cost: Free

www.minneapolisparks.org

Directions: Near 49th St., two blocks east of Hiawatha Ave.

Spooky Usher

If you find yourself seated on Aisle 18 at the Guthrie Theater, be prepared for an otherworldly experience. It's not what you might see on stage; it's what you might see right there in the aisle: a ghost!

The specter is the spirit of Richard Miller, a teenager who worked as an usher at the Guthrie during the 1960s. Miller was a pitiful Charlie Brown sort of fellow, unlucky in life and unluckier in love. He was teased unmercifully throughout high school, and the only place he found solace was at his job in the darkened theater.

Miller's college years were even worse. After suffering a nervous breakdown one semester, he missed his final exams. The ever-understanding college assigned him F's in all his courses. Distraught, Miller bought a gun and killed himself. His parents had him buried in his usher's uniform, a blue blazer with a red crest.

End of story? Hardly. Miller soon returned to his job at the Guthrie. Patrons began complaining about an usher walking around during performances, but nobody could find the guy with the telltale facial mole. Then somebody remembered: Miller had that same birthmark! Sometimes he appears as a misty haze near the ceiling, and sometimes he messes with the exit doors. If you see him at all, you'll probably think he works there.

Guthrie Theater, 725 Vineland Pl., Minneapolis, MN 55403

(877) 44-STAGE or (612) 377-2224

Hours: Call for hours

Cost: Performances vary

www.guthrietheater.org

Directions: Just west of Loring Park and I-94, where it turns into Hennepin Ave.

Tiny Tim's Death Site and Grave

November 30, 1996, was a sad day for music lovers everywhere. At a benefit concert at the Woman's Club of Minneapolis, Tiny Tim strummed "Tip-Toe Thru' the Tulips" on his ukulele for what turned out to be the last time. Midway through the song, the 64-year-old singer felt dizzy. He was helped back to his seat and collapsed in his wife's arms. It was the end of a strange, wonderful, 43-year career that included *Rowan and Martin's Laugh-In*, a 1969 marriage to Miss Vicki on the *Tonight Show* (that drew more television viewers than the first landing on the moon the same year), and a legion of diehard fans known as Tinyheads.

Tiny Tim was the stage name of Herbert Khaury, who, over the years, went by a variety of nicknames: Darry Dover, Julian Foxglove, Rollie Dell, Emmett Swink, and Larry Love, the Singing Canary. He started in Times Square in the 1950s reprising turn-of-the-century tunes for the crowd at Hubert's Museum and Live Flea Circus. He had a photographic memory for 100-year-old songs, thought aliens lived beneath the surface of the moon, and deeply admired Richard Nixon. And though many thought his warbling falsetto and eccentric behavior was an act, those close to him knew the truth: Tiny Tim in private was identical to Tiny Tim on stage.

When pressed about the details, the Woman's Club of Minneapolis is adamant about the role it *didn't* play in the crooner's death. First of all, they point out, Tiny Tim was at the fundraising event as a guest of his mother-in-law, and was definitely not hired to perform—he was drafted by guests. Secondly, though he dropped to the ground in the club, Tiny Tim was not technically declared dead until he arrived at the Hennepin County Medical Center (701 Park Ave.). OK, and JFK didn't die in Dealy Plaza. . . .

Woman's Club of Minneapolis, 410 Oak Grove St., Minneapolis, MN 55403

(612) 870-8001

Hours: Always visible; view from street

Cost: Free

www.womansclub.org

Directions: One Block south of W. 15th St., just east of I-94.

Fans turned out in droves for his open-casket funeral at the Basilica of St. Mary (88 N. 17th Street), as well as a hearse-chasing camera crew from the E! cable network. Tiny Tim was eulogized as an unwavering Christian and a unique American talent. He was buried with his ukulele, a stuffed rabbit, and six mauve tulips.

Lakewood Cemetery Mausoleum, 3600 Hennepin Ave., Minneapolis, MN 55408

(612) 822-2171

Hours: Daily 10 A.M.–4:30 P.M.

Cost: Free

Directions: Six blocks south of Lake St., eight blocks west of Lyndale Ave.; his crypt is on the lower level of the mausoleum; take a left coming out of the elevator and he's in the last alcove on the left.

St. Paul
Dillinger Lies Low

After John Dillinger escaped from jail in Crown Point, Indiana, on March 3, 1934, he fled to St. Paul with his girlfriend, Billie Frechette. Here he met up with Baby Face Nelson and asked him to join his new gang. Over the next few weeks they knocked off banks in Sioux Falls, South Dakota, and Mason City, Iowa, always returning to St. Paul.

Then, on March 31, 1934, the feds moved in on Dillinger while he was nursing a wound from an earlier gunshot. The FBI had been tipped off by the building's landlady. When two agents tried to enter through the front door they were met with a hail of gunfire. Dillinger was hit in the leg, but somehow managed to escape (yet again), mostly through the incompetence and bumbling of the St. Paul police and the federal agents. ("Watch both his getaway routes? Why would we do that?")

You'll get all the bloody details on the Dillinger fiasco, and much more, if you take the Gangster Tours run by Down in History Tours (see page 191) run out of the Wabasha Street Caves, a former mob hangout. At one time, St. Paul was notorious for police corruption and was a safe haven for criminals, so there are lots of stories to tell—it's a two-hour tour.

Lincoln Court Apartments, 93 S. Lexington Pkwy., Apartment 303, St. Paul, MN 55105

Private phone

Hours: Always visible; view from street

Cost: Free

Directions: On the corner of Lincoln Ave. and Lexington Pkwy., two blocks south of Summit Ave.

Just try that again!

The First American Shots in the Second World War

It was a definite case of too little, too late. On December 7, 1941, the USS *Ward* was patrolling the waters near the mouth of Pearl Harbor. The crew of Minnesota Naval Reservists spotted a midget submarine following another U.S. ship, so they fired on the craft. The first shot, from Gun #1, missed the sub, but the second shot, fired from Gun #3, hit the sub's conning tower. The Japanese vessel sank and was not found until August 2002.

Little did the *Ward* know, however, the submarine was being used to monitor the incoming attack. Everyone in Pearl Harbor would soon learn the truth. The USS *Ward* survived that day to be used in the South Pacific. It was hit by a kamikaze pilot in the Philippines three years later. The date? December 7, 1944, exactly three years to the day after the destroyer fired those first American shots in World War II.

Crews recovered Gun #3, and today it is mounted on the front lawn of the Minnesota State Capitol. If anyone plans another attack, they're ready. Let's just hope they do a better job this time.

State Capitol Building, 75 Constitution Ave., St. Paul, MN 55102

No phone

Hours: Always visible

Cost: Free

Directions: Between W. 12th St. and Constitution Ave. off John Ireland Blvd.

The Griggs Haunting

Chauncey Griggs built a 24-room mansion in 1883 with the money he made from his grocery empire, but the home became his ultimate curse . . . and the curse of a few others as well. A despondent, jilted maid hung herself from the fourth-floor landing, and things haven't been the same since.

A disembodied child's head floats above the beds. Windows open after they have been nailed shut. People stumble, as if tripped, on the stairs. Something gooses sleeping visitors. Dark men in top hats pass through walls and appear by guests' bedsides. Shadowy figures walk the stairs. A ghostly gardener is spotted in the library, flipping through the books. And Griggs himself appears in his Civil War uniform.

Every few years the place changes hands, usually sold to a nonbeliever. By the time the new owners unload it, they've been converted. The couple currently living there has no complaints . . . for the time being.

476 Summit Ave., St. Paul, MN 55102

Private phone

Hours: Always visible; view from street

Cost: Free

Directions: Two blocks west of the intersection of Summit Ave. and Ramsey St.

Hide in Plain Sight

Sara Jane Olson, by all accounts, was a model citizen. This soccer mom narrated the Christmas Pageant at the Minnehaha United Methodist Church, volunteered at a soup kitchen, taught English to immigrants, and even (no kidding) read to the blind.

Kathleen Ann Soliah, on the other hand, was a bit of a hothead. In 1975, as a member of the Symbionese Liberation Army, she reportedly planted pipe bombs under two LAPD squad cars in retaliation for the bloody shoot-out in Compton, California, a year earlier. Though indicted for the attempted bombing, Soliah disappeared in 1976 and was never captured. Then, after being featured on *America's Most Wanted*, a tip rolled in from St. Paul.

Sara Jane Olson was driving her Plymouth minivan in June 1999 when she was pulled over a mile from her posh home on Highland Avenue. FBI agent Mary Hogan approached the car and said, "FBI, Kathleen. It's over."

The news was certainly a blow to Olson/Soliah's three children, and probably a shock to her husband, Dr. Gerald "Fred" Peterson, as well. Her neighbors, who had dubbed her "Martha Stewart" (little did they know how right they were!), raised $1 million for her bail. For her part, Olson/Soliah started writing a cookbook after her arrest, *Serving Time: America's Most Wanted Recipes*, to raise money for her defense.

And she's needed it. Olson/Soliah pleaded guilty to the bombing charge and drew a 20-year sentence. She later claimed her confession was coerced, and as of this writing is up for appeal. Then, in January 2002, she was charged in the April 21, 1975, robbery of the Crocker National Bank in Carmichael, California, in which a mother of four was murdered. Three other former SLA members were also indicted. Patty "Tanya" Hearst admitted to driving the getaway car. (She's already done her time.) Olson/Soliah wasn't accused of pulling the trigger, but she was said to be in on the heist. All four SLA members pleaded guilty to second-degree murder in November 2002.

Many of Olson/Soliah's old friends and neighbors thought bygones should be bygones—youthful indiscretions—at least on the bombing attempt. After all, wasn't she a fabulous cook? A dedicated car-pooler? A faithful recycler? Hadn't she repaid her debt to society by being such an upstanding citizen? But if that were solid reasoning, shouldn't more of the folks on the FBI's Ten Most Wanted list start brushing up on their soufflés?

Arrest Site, Edgcumbe & Niles, St. Paul, MN 55116

No phone

Hours: Always visible

Cost: Free

Directions: Two blocks south of Randolph Ave., two blocks west of I-35 E.

THE WORLD ACCORDING TO JESSE

Jesse Ventura is no longer the governor of Minnesota, but he left his mark. He will be missed by oddballs everywhere. Thankfully he generated a wealth of original musings on public policy:

Political Strategy: "Win if you can, lose if you must, but always cheat." (From a speech to a college crowd.)

The Arts: "I tried to listen to [*A Prairie Home Companion*] once, but I fell asleep."

Gun Control: "If you can put two rounds into the same hole from 25 meters, that's gun control!"

City Planning: "Whoever designed the streets [of St. Paul] must have been drunk . . . I think it was those Irish guys."

Health Care: "Every fat person says it's not their fault, and that they have gland trouble. You know what gland? The saliva gland. They can't push away from the table."

Civil Disobedience: Ventura joined the antiwar movement while he was a Navy SEAL because "I loved the braless thing. I'm very heterosexual. I'd see women out burning their bras and I'd go over with a lighter: 'Can I help you?'"

Religion: Organized religion is "for the weak-minded."

Life After Death: Admitted that he wants to be reincarnated as a 38DD bra.

Public Discourse: "If I don't know and I believe it's so because it's so, then it's so."

Peanuts Town

Though it was never revealed where the characters in the comic strip *Peanuts* lived, it can be safely assumed that they lived in St. Paul. That's because its creator Charles Schulz was, by all accounts, Charlie Brown. Charlie Brown's father was a barber; so was Schulz's. Charlie Brown had an unrequited crush on a redhead; ditto for Schulz. Charlie Brown had a dog named Snoopy, as did Schulz. Charlie Brown was a lovable loser; Schulz made millions of dollars.

OK, so the parallel stops somewhere, but who wants to read a comic strip about a boy who achieved worldwide fame and fortune?

Charles Schulz was born November 26, 1922, in Minneapolis and was nicknamed Sparky after Barney Google's horse, Spark Plug. His father ran the Family Barber Shop in St. Paul (Snelling Avenue and Selby Street) and the family rented a home nearby (473 Macalister Street). Sparky attended St. Paul's Central High School where his cartoons were rejected for publication by his high school yearbook. The shy teenager began taking art classes from the Art Instruction Schools, a correspondence school known for it's "Draw Me" matchbook advertisements. In a course called "Drawing of Children," Schulz got a C+.

Despite his early stumbles, Schulz went on to work for the Art Instruction Schools grading papers. It was here that he met, and was rejected by, red-haired Donna Johnson (later Donna Wold) from accounting. He never got over the loss. Moonlighting, he inked lettering for a Catholic cartoon magazine called *Timeless Topix*, and later submitted one-cell cartoons to the *Saturday Evening Post*. He sold 15 of them, which helped him sell a four-cell strip called *Li'l Folks* to the *St. Paul Pioneer Press* in 1947. The strip was picked up by United Feature Syndicate three years later and renamed *Peanuts*. Schulz thought the new name sounded insignificant, and hated it to his dying day.

Schulz died in California on February 12, 2000, the night before his final Sunday comic was scheduled to run. His death hasn't stopped the franchise, and Schulz continues to make millions year after year. The town of St. Paul has hosted several *Peanuts*-themed art events. In the summer of 2000, 101 differently painted fiberglass Snoopys were placed around the city. The following summer it was Charlie Browns. More celebrations are planned, with the goal of erecting a permanent bronze statue to Schulz. Not too bad for a former blockhead.

St. Paul Convention and Visitors Bureau, PO Box 516, St. Paul, MN 55102

(800) 574-2150 or (952) 445-1660

Hours: Call for information

Cost: Free

www.stpaulcvb.org

Directions: Call for directions.

You ought to have your head examined.

Questionable Medical Devices

Years ago, Bob McCoy started "a museum dedicated to lies, deceptions, and mistruths (not to be confused with the Nixon Library)." The Museum of Questionable Medical Devices grew to be the world's most comprehensive collection of quackery. Among its artifacts:

• **Battle Creek Vibratory Chair** (early 1900s). Its jackhammer-like vibrations were said to relieve constipation. Patients sat on the chair for a half hour, then followed it up with a yogurt enema.

• **Omnipotent Oscilloclast** (1920s). The thinly disguised Japanese shortwave radio would cure you of any ailment after testing the frequency of one of your bodily fluids.

- **Foot X-ray Machine** (1940s and '50s). This radioactive x-ray device was used in shoe stores to determine the ideal fit for a shoe by observing the buyer's bones. Its use was finally banned in 1970.
- **G-H-R Electric Thermitis Dilator** (also known as the Prostate Warmer) (1918). Plug it in twice—one end into an electrical socket and the other into you—and it would stimulate your "abnormal brain" to 100°F. It was said to cure impotence.
- **MacGregor Rejuvenator.** Guaranteed to reverse the aging process with radio, infrared, and ultraviolet waves in an iron lung–like chamber.
- **Electro-Metabograph.** Its inventor claimed it could cure patients of such ailments as the desire to kill, homesickness, and overactive sexual desire.

The visitors' favorite, however, was the Psychograph Phrenology Machine (circa 1905). For a mere $3, a museum staff member would fit a cage over your head so that small pegs could measure the bumps on your skull for such traits as sexamity, constructiveness, sublimity, suavity, amativeness, and causality. It was a bargain at any price.

When McCoy decided to retire in 2001, the Science Museum of Minnesota stepped up to the plate and offered to build a special exhibit for the collection, which is where you can find the artifacts today. You can still have your head examined.

Science Museum of Minnesota, 120 W. Kellogg Blvd., St. Paul, MN 55102
(651) 221-9444

Hours: June–August, Monday–Saturday 9:30 A.M.–9 P.M., Sunday 10:30 A.M. –5:30 P.M.;
September–May, Monday–Saturday 9:30 A.M.–7 P.M., Sunday 10:30 A.M.–5:30 P.M.
Cost: Adults $7, Kids $5
www.smm.org/visitorinfo/planyourtrip/tour/Collections.php
Directions: Three blocks west of Wabasha St. on Kellogg Blvd., at the river.

ST. PAUL
F. Scott Fitzgerald was born at 481 Laurel Avenue on September 24, 1896. A statue of the famous author stands today in nearby Rice Park (St. Peter and Market Streets).

Tacky, tacky, tacky!

Twin Towns Tacky Tour

If you've gotten this far in this book, you've already demonstrated an affection for bad taste, so why not go whole hog on the Twin Towns Tacky Tour? Hosted by the Gunderson sisters (who, depending on your tour, are not always biologically female), you'll pass a few of the sites mentioned in this book . . . and so much more. The tour route is always changing, but you're likely to see such things as the world's first Target store, the Ramsey County Pet Cemetery, a Falcon Heights boulder that marks the halfway point between the equator and the North Pole, and several winners of the ugliest architecture awards. The sisters will regale you with stories of romantic trips to White Castle for Valentine's Day and visits to the Minnesota State Fair to see high art—chainsaw sculptures and butter carvings—all with thick Midwestern/Scandinavian accents, don'tcha know. The tour takes about two hours, unless the Gundersons spot a garage sale—and boy can they spot 'em! Yah, you betcha!

Down in History Tours offers a wide variety of trips, including gangster tours of both St. Paul and Minneapolis, excursions deep into the Wabasha Street Caves and the Joseph Wolf Caves in Stillwater, and a Rivers and Roots tour along the Mississippi. Your guides are always costumed actors who are extremely familiar with local history.

Down in History Tours, Wabasha Street Caves, 215 S. Wabasha St., St. Paul, MN 55107
(651) 292-1220
Hours: Every other Saturday, 2:30 P.M.; call for times
Cost: $20
www.wabashastreetcaves.com
Directions: Tours depart from the Wabasha Street Caves, just across the river from downtown St. Paul.

ST. PAUL
St. Paul was founded by **Pierre "Pig's Eye" Parrant**, who built a cabin here in 1838. The settlement was known as Pig's Eye until 1849.

Amelia Earhart lived with her family at 825 Fairmount Avenue from 1913 to 1915, during her first years in high school.

Chief Sitting Bull was almost assassinated outside the Grand Opera House in St. Paul on September 4, 1884.

Suburbs
Bloomington
Louis Farrakhan on the One-Woman Hit List

You can hardly blame Qubilah Shabazz for being angry. At the age of four she saw her father, Malcolm X, gunned down before her very eyes. Some pointed the finger at those close to Louis Farrakhan, and apparently Qubilah was in that camp . . . or at least was tempted into that way of thinking by Michael Fitzpatrick, a so-called friend.

Some friend. Fitzpatrick wore an FBI wire in 1995 as Shabazz negotiated the final details in a Bloomington hotel room to have Farrakhan eliminated. During the meeting she turned over $250 as a down payment, which was all the FBI needed to arrest her.

Fitzpatrick, it should be noted, hardly had a clean reputation himself; he appeared to be cooperating with the FBI to save his own skin on other charges. It looked like Shabazz was being set up. The case was eventually dismissed when Shabazz accepted responsibility for the events and enrolled in a chemical-dependency program. Farrakhan rushed to defend Shabazz claiming it was a government conspiracy to discredit him, at best, and assassinate him, at worst.

Holiday Inn Express, 814 E. 79th St., Bloomington, MN 55420

(952) 854-5558

Hours: Always visible

Cost: Free; rooms $109 and up

www.basshotels.com/hiexpress?_franchisee=MSPEX

Directions: Take the Portland Ave. Exit from I-494, go south one block, turn east on 79th St., one block ahead at Chicago Ave.

Mall of America

All right, all right—so the Mall of America isn't exactly the most off-the-beaten-path tourist destination. By some accounts, the MOA gets more visitors each year than Disneyland, Graceland, and the Grand Canyon *combined*. But you have to admit—it is odd.

For example, look at the mall itself. Built on the site of the old Metropolitan Stadium, it has 4.2 million square feet of floor space. That means you could fit 32 747s, 9 Eiffel Towers, and Mt. Rushmore inside—at the same time! Not counting the four flagship stores (Macy's, Bloomingdale's,

Nordstrom, and Sears), it contains more than 400 specialty shops. In other words, if you spent one minute—a mere 60 seconds—in each and every store, it would take you more than an eight-hour day to see them all, and that's with no breaks at the food court. The MOA is laid out on a square floor plan, four floors tall, where each lap is six-tenths of a mile.

And you want to know what's even stranger? It's not even the world's largest—the West Edmonton Mall in Alberta, Canada, is larger!

Mall of America, 81st St. & Cedar Ave., Bloomington, MN 55425

(952) 883-8800

Hours: Monday–Saturday, 10 A.M.–9:30 P.M., Sunday 11 A.M.–7 P.M.

Cost: Free

www.mallofamerica.com

Directions: Exit Rte. 494 at Cedar Ave. or 24th Ave. and head south—it's hard to miss.

The MOA wraps around Camp Snoopy, billed as the largest indoor theme park in America. The seven-acre park is built within a transplanted forest. Take a ride on Paul Bunyan's Log Chute past animatronic logging camp scenes. Have a seat in the Mighty Ax, where you're swung upside down in a six-story arc. Or ride the Ripsaw Rollercoaster above the treetops.

Camp Snoopy, 5000 Center Court, Bloomington, MN 55425

(952) 883-8600

Hours: Daily 10 A.M.–9:30 P.M.

Cost: Free; rides, $22 all-day pass

www.campsnoopy.com

Directions: In the middle of the Mall of America.

Still looking for something to do? How about the newest addition: Cereal Adventure! (www.cerealadventure.com, (952) 814-2900) Its slogan? "Where Your Favorite Cereals Come to Life!" They've got the Cocoa Puffs Chocolate Canyon, the Lucky Charms Magical Forest, the Trix Fruity Carnival, and the Cheerios Play Park. And all these folks charge you to attend this General Mills walk-through commercial is $3.95 a head.

Looking for something a little less corporate and a little more educational? Try Underwater Adventures (www.underwateradventures.com, (952) 883-0202). Here you'll travel beneath the waves through Plexiglas tunnels to see sharks, turtles, and stingrays. If you want to get a little closer, they'll even let you pet a shark.

And if you really want to cement the MOA visit in your memory, bring your significant other to the Chapel of Love. Though it has been condemned by the archbishop of Minneapolis/St. Paul, more than 2,500 couples—1,250 of them happy—can't be wrong! The nation's only mall-based wedding chapel has pew space for 75 guests—more for those willing to listen to the service piped into the gift shop.

The Chapel of Love was the final destination in the Campaign to Elect a Mrs. David Weinlick on June 13, 1998. Weinlick's friends held a competition to choose him a mate, and 27 women vied for the position. Winner Elizabeth Runze was selected in front of 3,000 spectators. She marched to the chapel with the man she had just met and tied the knot. How romantic!

Chapel of Love, 240 N. Garden, Bloomington, MN 55425
(800) 299-LOVE
Hours: Call to schedule a ceremony
Cost: Dream Wedding $195; Mega-Wedding $3,295
www.chapeloflove.com
Directions: On the third level, southeast corner, next to Bloomingdale's.

Burnsville
Fantasuite Motel

Minnesota winters can be mighty drab, so if you find yourself with a budding case of cabin fever, there's a place you can go to get away from it all and never leave the state! A Caribbean island, a gondola in Venice, a pharaoh's tomb . . . and they're all under one roof: the Fantasuite Motel in Burnsville.

Though this Ramada has standard rooms, for about $100 more you can be whisked away to the overnight destination of your dreams. Feeling a little Cro-Magnon? Drag your mate into Le Cave, where the bed is framed by stalactites and a waterfall feeds a whirlpool. Maybe you've got a Jonah fetish—so why not try out Moby Dick, where your waterbed is in a dinghy and the whirlpool is in the great whale's mouth? Or climb up to the Tree House, where your bed is suspended from four sturdy oaks, and it swings. Arabian Nights, Jungle Safari, Space Odyssey, Wild Wild West, Cinderella, Log Cabin, and Sherwood Forest are much as you'd expect. Finally, if you find yourself missing the snow during the three months each year when you can't find it, there's always the Northern Lights: a 7-foot round waterbed awaits you in your own private igloo.

Ramada Limited, 250 N. River Ridge Circle, Burnsville, MN 55337

(800) 666-STAY or (952) 890-9550

Hours: Always open; Tours Saturday–Sunday 3 P.M.

Cost: $149–$199

www.fantasuite.com

Directions: Head east on Rte. 13 from I-35 W, take a left at the first stoplight, and left at the second street in the office park.

Eagan
The 20th Hijacker

In the coulda, shoulda, woulda world of post–September 11 America, it's easy to come down on intelligence agencies who missed what was a vast terrorist conspiracy. Everyone wants to be a Monday morning FBI agent. What cannot be denied, however, was that some folks were on the ball and had an inkling that something terrible was brewing—it's tragic that others didn't heed their warnings.

First up for praise are the flight instructors at Pan-Am International, a flight school in suburban Eagan. French-born Zacarias Moussaoui showed up at the school in the summer of 2001 asking for flight training on a Boeing 747. He claimed to have no previous piloting experience with any type of aircraft, much less with the largest commercial airliner in the world. What's more, he didn't want to know how to take off or land, just to steer it once it was aloft. When he paid the $6,300 fee up front, in cash, the school called the FBI. It took six calls for their warnings to be taken seriously.

While the INS held Moussaoui on visa violations, FBI agents tracked him back to another flight school in Oklahoma. It was the same school attended by Al Qaeda operative Abdul Hakim Murad, a man who testified in the 1996 trial of Ramsi Yusef, accused and later convicted of masterminding the 1993 World Trade Center bombing. Murad claimed he was training to fly a planeful of explosives into the CIA headquarters.

Top brass at the FBI received information from French authorities in late August that Moussaoui was also part of Al Qaeda, yet they still would not allow Minneapolis agents to search the contents of the detainee's home computer. Field agents tried desperately to get the FBI to take the threat seriously, but to no avail.

After September 11, FBI director Robert Mueller denied the agency had previous knowledge of terrorists training in the United States. Enter Coleen Rowley. This respected Minneapolis field agent wrote a scathing 13-page letter criticizing FBI headquarters and their internal ass-covering culture and suggesting that it might have been possible to stop the attacks had the leads played out. When Rowley testified on Capitol Hill, President Bush rolled out a previously unheard-of restructuring of the federal government at the same hour she was speaking to Congress, which upstaged her testimony completely.

Pan-Am International Flight Academy, 2915 Commers Dr., Eagan, MN 55121
(651) 681-8190

Hours: Always visible; view from street

Cost: Free

Directions: Just south of the Dodd Rd. (Rte. 149) intersection with Rte. 55.

ANOKA
Anoka claims to be the Halloween Capital of the World. Each October the town puts a neon jack-o-lantern atop city hall.

COON RAPIDS
In 1957, several children around Coon Rapids told their parents they had seen a "big bunny." Adults laughed off the kids' stories, until later that same year when Barbara Battmer, a respectable local woman, spotted a pair of kangaroos. They were seen again near the Anoka County Fairground in 1967.

GOLDEN VALLEY
When Golden Valley Christian radio station KYCR went off the air for two days for repairs, some local listeners thought the Rapture had begun. That, or "the government had outlawed Christian broadcasting."

Do you have to remind us?

North St. Paul
World's Largest Snowman

You'd think with all the winter weather this region endures, folks around here would be happy to forget the snow and subzero temperatures for a few months each summer. Well, forget that notion if you're in North St. Paul, because they've built the World's Largest Snowman, and he's up year-round!

The secret to the 54-foot Frosty's longevity is that he's made of stucco, not snow. Designed by Lloyd Koesling, he was erected downtown in 1974 by the local Jaycees for the annual Sno-Daze celebration. The festival is a not-so-subtle rip-off of the Winter Carnival celebrated by a certain larger city to the immediate south. The supersized snowman has two large black buttons; look closely and you'll see they aren't buttons, but speakers that pump out holiday music. If you stop by in December, this will be obvious.

The landmark was moved to its present location in 1992 and refurbished. He was given a fresh coat of paint and a tattoo with "Painted by Dick the Painter" on his rump. Some think the statue is partially anatomically correct, but that small door on his rear does not evacuate ice cubes; it's only the entrance to a storage shed within.

Centennial St. (Rte. 36) & Margaret St., North St. Paul, MN 55109

No phone

Hours: Always visible

Cost: Free

Directions: On the intersection's southeast corner, in Rotary Park, two long blocks east of McKnight Rd.

St. Louis Park
Pavek Museum of Broadcasting

Among the many factual errors in the movie *Titanic* is the scene in which a radio operator sends out a distress signal after the ocean liner strikes the iceberg. The operator feverishly taps out an S.O.S. message, trying to locate ships in the vicinity. "It might have worked better had they turned the transmitter on," your tour guide offers before firing up the museum's 1912 rotary spark-gap transmitter. The guide punches out the same distress signal, but the tapping is drowned out by the crackle of high-powered sparks, and you're overcome with the sweet smell of ozone. "That's why early radio operators were nicknamed 'Sparky', and where the term 'take a breather' came from," you're told.

That's just the start of your radio education at the Pavek Museum of Broadcasting. The museum is filled with hundreds of radios, phonographs, microphones, speakers, antennae, televisions, tape recorders, vacuum tubes, and camera cranes. Most are in working order, as your guide will demonstrate, and no doubt you'll be a little annoyed that a 1950s magnetic tape recorder can still deliver clear sound when the VCR you bought a year ago is already on the fritz.

The Pavek Museum approaches its educational mission with the zeal of a tent revival. It offers weekend classes for budding broadcasters. There is an extensive library of technical manuals for electronics hobbyists looking to restore their garage sale finds. The museum is a popular field trip for local schools, and for a very good reason: it's a lot of fun.

3515 Raleigh Ave., St. Louis Park, MN 55416

(952) 926-8198

Hours: Tuesday–Friday 10 A.M.–6 P.M., Saturday 9 A.M.–5 P.M.

Cost: Adults $5, Seniors $3, Kids $3

www.pavekmuseum.org

Directions: One block east of Rte. 100 on W. 36th St., turn north on Raleigh Ave.

Stillwater
The Younger Brothers in Jail

After confessing to taking part in the failed Northfield Bank raid, the three Younger Brothers were sentenced to life in prison at Stillwater. (Because they pleaded guilty, state law prevented their execution.) Bob Younger died there of tuberculosis on September 16, 1889. Jim and Cole turned out to be model prisoners; Cole even started the *Prison Mirror*, a Big House newspaper that is still published to this day (but out of the Sandstone correctional facility). Jesse James reportedly contributed $50 to his old cohort to get it started.

The surviving pair served 25 years before the Minnesota legislature, finally buying into the Civil-War-made-'em-do-it defense, released them in July 1901 on the condition they not leave the state. They moved to St. Paul and sold tombstones. A fawning newspaper reporter who lobbied for the pair's release wanted to marry Jim, but the parole board refused the request. Distraught, Jim committed suicide in St. Paul's Reardon Hotel (7th and Minnesota Streets) on October 19, 1902.

Cole was granted a full pardon by the governor in 1903, but this time the conditions required that he leave the state, so he returned to Missouri. There he teamed up with the raid's only surviving member, Frank James, to tour the lecture circuit giving cautionary high-drama speeches on the dangers of a life of crime. He died of heart failure on March 21, 1916, at the age of 72. He was buried with 17 bullets still in his body.

The only remaining structure from the old Stillwater Prison, the Warden's House, is a museum today. In addition to local history, there is a small room dedicated to the Youngers and other prisoners at Stillwater.

The Warden's Home Museum, 602 N. Main St., PO Box 167, Stillwater, MN 55082
(651) 439-5956
Hours: Tuesday, Thursday, Saturday, Sunday 2–5 P.M.
Cost: Adults $3, Kids (6–17) $1
www.wchsmn.org
Directions: Along the river, north of the bridge, on Rte. 36/95 (Main St.).

White Bear Lake
World's Largest Polar Bear

Minnesota is not north of the Arctic Circle, though it might be hard to convince visitors otherwise in February. It's an even harder task if the visitors are in White Bear Lake, because sitting atop a Chevrolet dealership is the World's Largest Polar Bear. He was created out of fiberglass in 1964 by Gordon Shumaker for a local car dealership. When Thane Hawkins Polar Chevrolet opened its new dealership in 1989, the enormous ursine was mounted atop the new building. The gigantic creature is modest but patriotic: it wears a pair of red, white, and blue boxer shorts.

The town of White Bear Lake is named for a local Native American legend about a ghost white bear living on an island in the nearby lake.

Thane Hawkins Polar Chevrolet, 1801 E. County Road F, White Bear Lake, MN 55110
(651) 429-7791
Hours: Always visible
Cost: Free
Directions: At the intersection of Rte. F and Rte. 61.

6

THE BIG FISH TOUR

You didn't think you were going to get through a Minnesota travel guide without any reference to fishing, did you? Next to talking about the weather, fishing is the state's favorite pastime.

And, boy, do Minnesotans take the sport seriously. Look at the town of Aiken: each November, on the day after Thanksgiving, residents have a Fish House Parade down Main Street to kick off ice-fishing season. Nobody was laughing a few years ago, though, when 19 late-in-the-season fishermen, trapped on a melting ice floe, drifted a half-mile into Lake Mille Lacs! Luckily, there's no danger of a similar mishap happening in Walker during its annual International Eelpout Festival—that's because the event is held in February when nothing melts. Contestants vie for the trophy for the World's Ugliest Fish, which by definition is the largest eelpout pulled from a local lake.

Now I'll be honest, I'm not a big fishing fan. I consider the hours I've spent staring at a bobber waiting for a strike as . . . well . . . hours spent, nothing more. I am, however, a big fan of big fish. By that I mean BIG fish. Perhaps the desire to return to the office on Monday morning with an outrageous fish story is hardwired into all human brains—even mine. I just don't want to go through the trouble of impaling a worm on a hook to come up with the story.

So whether you enjoy the sport or not, this themed tour is for you, from how to choose your tackle to landing the big one. With just a little trick photography, you too can bring back shots of the one that got away to impress the folks around the water cooler.

Pequot Lakes
World's Largest Bobber

Now where do you find a 120-foot fishing pole?

First things first: You can't go fishing for the world's largest fish without the proper equipment, and let's face it, it's tough to come by a bobber that's 60 feet in diameter in your local tackle shop. For that, you have to go to Pequot Lakes.

The World's Largest Bobber (Paul Bunyan's Bobber) has loomed over this fishing community for years. The town uses the red-and-white ball as a water tower. The bobber is illuminated after dark, so you should have no problem locating it, day or night.

Chamber of Commerce, PO Box 208, Pequot Lakes, MN 56472

(218) 568-8911

Hours: Always visible

Cost: Free

www.pequotlakes.com/legend.cfm

Directions: Just west of the stoplight along Rte. 371, in the center of town.

Pelland Junction
Willie the Worm Man

Tackle in hand, you'll need bait. Big bait. If you're using worms, there's none bigger than Willie the Worm Man, a six-foot spineless mutant hanging from a hook outside the "Y" Bar in Pelland Junction, just southwest of International Falls.

Yeah, yeah, it sounds like a dirty joke—come and see the six-foot Willie!—but he's for real. Willie is actually a chainsaw sculpture, not a true wriggler, but the fish won't realize that until it's too late. And because he's more of a lure than a worm, you can reuse him on your next outing. Remember to bring a pretty big sinker; he's made of wood and won't go down easily. A bowling ball ought to do the trick.

"Y" Bar, 5536 Hwy. 11, Pelland Junction, MN 56649

(218) 283-8879

Hours: Always visible

Cost: Free

Directions: Just east of the intersection of Rtes. 71 and 11.

Big Willie.

Baudette
World's Largest Walleye

One of Minnesota's favorite sport fishes is the walleye, so much so that it's the official state fish. If you're angling for big walleyes, you have three choices. The first is the largest: Willie Walleye. (Not to be confused with Willie the Worm Man.) He's 40 feet long and weighs in at 9,852 pounds. Willie was made in 1959 by Arnold Lund, using an iron skeleton with stucco scales.

The folks in Baudette are mighty fond of Willie; they throw a celebration in his honor each June: Willie Walleye Day! They also call their town the Walleye Capital of the World. Once you see their Willie, it's hard to argue the point.

Unfortunately, to get to Willie you have to damn near drive to Canada to see him. Isn't there a humongous walleye that's a little closer?

International Dr., Baudette, MN 56623

(800) 382-FISH

Hours: Always visible

Cost: Free

www.lakeofthewoodsmn.com/attractions/willie.html

Directions: On Rte. 11 (International Dr.) overlooking Baudette Bay, just south of the U.S.–Canada border.

Hop on up!

Ray
Ride That Walleye!

Another walleye, smaller than Willie but located a heck of a lot closer to civilization, can be found near Ray. What's more, the folks in this resort community know who's boss, and it ain't the fish. Baudettians might worship their world-record walleye, but here in Ray, they've strapped a saddle on their statue for folks to ride! Now who's top of the food chain, hmmmmm?

The idea for a bronco-riding bigmouth came to Duane Beyers in 1949. He built the 16-foot walleye near the entrance to Lake Kabetogama and placed a staircase behind the fish for easy access. Don't worry if you're a tenderfoot, the statue doesn't buck, and nobody who sees your picture will be able to tell from a photograph whether or not you are really riding a moving critter. Trust me.

Rtes. 53 & 122, Ray, MN 56669

No phone

Hours: Always visible

Cost: Free

www.kabetogama.com

Directions: Six miles east of town on Rte. 53, at the Rte. 122 turnoff.

No saddle on this one.

Garrison
Big Walleye

If you think it's insulting to treat the state fish as if it's a horse or to give it a silly human name, perhaps the 15-foot walleye in Garrison will be more to your liking. It's also an easy drive from the Twin Cities. The Garrison fish is definitely the most anatomically accurate walleye of the bunch, if you're looking for realism. And something else: it's mobile!

The statue was installed along the shore of Lake Mille Lacs in 1980. Though it appears to rest firmly on a pedestal, its base isn't permanent.

When Garrison has a fishy celebration, they lift this fiberglass walleye onto a flatbed and away they go. Sure, this poses a risk with prank-minded teenagers around, but it's a risk these Garrison folk are willing to take.

Central St. & Rte. 169, Garrison, MN 56450

No phone

Hours: Always visible

Cost: Free

Directions: At Lake Mille Lacs, two blocks south of the Rte. 18 intersection on Rte. 169.

Don't let it get back into the lake!

Erskine
World's Largest Northern Pike

If you're not partial to walleye, and northern pike is more your speed, drop on by the eastern shore of Lake Cameron in Erskine. There you'll find a 20-foot concrete pike headed for the water. It's an old pike—it only has four teeth left—having been built in 1953 by local artist Ernie Konickson.

Erskine's northern pike isn't just for those who like to fish. If you're the type who wishes that sometimes the fish could win the age-old battle with humans, you can pose for a photo with your head in its gaping mouth.

City Park, Vance Ave. & 2nd St., Erskine, MN 56535

No phone

Hours: Always visible

Cost: Free

Directions: Two blocks south of Rte. 2 on Rte. 34 (Vance Ave.).

Ready for a fish fry.

Nevis
World's Largest Tiger Muskie—Not

The folks of Nevis are pretty proud of their tiger muskie, so much so that they've proclaimed it to be the world's largest. Well, perhaps that was true in 1950 when Warren Ballard built the 30.5-foot-long fish out of wood and cement—Minnesota's governor even came to dedicate the statue when it was unveiled on the shore of Lake Belle Taine—but all that was before the Space Race.

No, not the Outer Space Race. The Civic Space Race. Nevis was bested by an evil empire to the east . . . Wisconsin. In 1976, a 143-foot-long fiberglass tiger muskie was erected in Hayward, Wisconsin, and it wasn't just the World's Largest Tiger Muskie, it was the World's Largest

Fiberglass *Anything*. Today, visitors could walk through a door in its side and march up a flight of steps to pose in its open mouth!

In the end, there was just no way Nevis could compete. The townspeople eventually moved their muskie, placing it beneath a protective shelter along the main drag. It still bears its now-outdated sign, like Gerald Ford strutting around demanding he still be called Mr. President. It's just sad . . .

Bunyan Trails Rd. & Main St., PO Box FISH-E, Nevis, MN 56467

(800) 332-FISH

Hours: Always visible

Cost: Free

www.nevis.govoffice.com

Directions: Three blocks north of Rte. 34 on Rte. 2 (Bunyan Trails Rd.).

Just add lye.

Madison
Lou T. Fisk

The trouble with posing with big fiberglass fish that resemble big sport fish is that the real-fish-to-fake-fish ratio isn't as large as it would be for, say, the World's Largest Minnow. If you want to impress others with a small fish gone large, stop by Madison, home of Lou T. Fisk, the World's Largest Codfish.

Madison bills itself as Lutefisk Capital, USA. Each November the town hosts a lutefisk-eating contest during Norsefest. For those of you unfamiliar with this Norwegian delicacy, lutefisk is dried cod soaked in lye to the consistency of wallpaper paste. Each year some out-of-town sucker is talked into participating in the contest, and each year that goo-eating fool comes in a queasy fifth or sixth place. Don't be that victim: lutefisk is nasty. Call it a tradition. Call it an acquired taste. It's still vile, vile, vile.

Needless to say, the best time to see the big fish in Madison is between December and October. Lou is a 25-foot, pre-lutefisk codfish, and is the town's official mascot. The fiberglass creature cost $8,000 and was dedicated in 1983. When asked about the project, a local booster admitted why the town shelled out 8 G's: "We don't think you can very well ignore a 25-foot codfish."

They were right about that one.

J. F. Jacobson Park, 100 S. 8th Ave., Madison, MN 56256

(320) 598-7373 ext. 14

Hours: Always visible

Cost: Free

www.madisonmn.org

Directions: Just south of the Rte. 4 intersection with Rte. 75 (8th Ave.).

Orr
Big Bluefish

Compared to giant walleyes, northern pikes, muskies, and even codfish, bluefish seem kind of . . . well . . . puny. Even this five-by-ten-foot bluefish built by Gordon Shumaker doesn't quite measure up.

But you're a lot more likely to land a bluefish than a muskie if you're fishing in these parts, so if the ultimate goal is to fool your coworkers, you might want to come to Orr. You probably don't stand a chance telling them you reeled in a 40-foot walleye, but a bluefish a quarter of that size? It's worth a shot.

Rte. 23 & Rte. 53, Orr, MN 55771

No phone

Hours: Always visible

Cost: Free

Directions: On the south end of town.

Trout on wheels.

Preston
Big Brown Trout

When you get to the southern part of Minnesota, the lakes get smaller and farther between. So do the fish. But you can find trout—brown trout—if you look hard enough. You're sure to reel one in if you stop by the town of Preston, which has two very large fish. The first is six feet long and was carved with a chainsaw by Barry Pinske in 1987. It sits in front of City Hall. The other is made of fiberglass and is three times longer—19 feet from snout to tailfin. It sits on a flatbed that can be pulled around town during Preston Trout Days each year.

Kansas St. & Minnesota Rd., Preston, MN 55965

(888) 845-2100 or (507) 765-2100

Hours: Always visible

Cost: Free

www.bluffcountry.com/preston.htm

Directions: Just south of Rte. 52 (Kansas St.) on Minnesota Rd., at the north end of town.

For those with a Jonah complex.

Bena
Big Fish Supper Club

Assuming you've been able to pull off one of the previous big fish lies, why not try for something a little bigger? Set your sights on a restaurant west of Bena: the Big Fish Supper Club.

The eatery's tables are actually located in a building adjacent to this 65-foot-long muskellunge fronting the road. The fish was constructed in 1958 by stretching tarpaper over wooden ribs. In the beginning it was a hamburger and sandwich stand where brave patrons stepped into the fish's mouth to retrieve their dinners. Then it was converted into a souvenir hut. But no more. Today it's used as a storage shed for the restaurant. What a shame.

To the club's credit, the big fish has been well-painted and maintained. Considering what it's made of, it's amazing it's still standing more than 40+ years later. But wouldn't it be a lot more exciting to have a table inside the belly of the beast, especially if you have a Jonah complex?

456 Rte. 2 East, Bena, MN 56626

(218) 665-2333

Hours: Always visible

Cost: Free

Directions: One mile west of town on Rte. 2.

Only half a fish.

Mounds View Mermaid!

If you were able to snow your friends with the Bena fish, why not try to tell them you caught something realllllllly amazing: a half-fish, half-woman mermaid! You can find a 30-foot specimen atop the Mermaid Entertainment and Convention Center in suburban Mounds View. It was built of fiberglass in 1967 by Robert Johnson as an advertisement for the Mermaid Supper Club. Over time the business expanded to include a bowling alley and a large meeting hall.

Ask anyone for directions in Mounds View and you'll likely hear the mermaid mentioned as a landmark: " . . . and take a left at the mermaid." Nobody seems to appreciate the irony that a town named Mounds View has a bare-breasted statue as its best-known piece of public art.

Mermaid Entertainment and Convention Center, 2200 Rte. 10, Mounds View, MN 55112

(763) 784-7350

Hours: Always visible

Cost: Free

Directions: East of Rte. 8 on Rte. H, just past Rte. 10.

Crosby's Nessie.

Crosby
Sea Serpent!!

OK, it's not exactly the Loch Ness monster, but it's the best damn fish story you'll find in Minnesota. Native American legends have long spoken of a creature named Kanabec living in what is now called Serpent Lake. Or at the very least, local boosters have spoken of Native American legends that reportedly mention a creature living in the lake. That's right, the stories are likely a hoax dreamed up by the chamber of commerce.

The town erected a statue to their nonmonster in 1977, and the myth has endured in spite of a marked lack of evidence. The fiberglass creature is 20 feet tall and appears to have crawled onto the shore. It might have made more sense to mount the statue in the lake—at least anglers and tourists could snap a photo and claim to have spotted something.

Crosby Memorial Park, 4th St. & Rte. 210, Crosby, MN 56441

No phone

Hours: Always visible

Cost: Free

Directions: At the west end of Serpent Lake, four blocks south of the Rte. 6 intersection.

EPiLOGUE

*F*irst the good news: Minnesota deserves a round of applause for all it has done to create, preserve, and restore its roadside wonders. When the folks of Frazee accidentally torched their giant fiberglass turkey, a new gobbler rose like a phoenix before the end of the year. When a freak windstorm in Hackensack blew the head off LucetteDiana Kensack, Paul Bunyan's sweetheart, another noggin was installed atop her Amazonian frame—and a much prettier head at that! And when the Minneapolis Museum of Questionable Medical Devices closed its doors, the Science Museum of Minnesota stepped up to save the Psychograph Phrenology Machine, the Omnipotent Oscilloclast, and the Radium Suppositories.

But now the bad news: not every attraction has been so lucky. The three-foot tall jackalope statue outside a monument company in Sleepy Eye is now extinct. Spicer's Safari South Restaurant, where hundreds of animal heads stared down on you while you ate, has been converted to a more tasteful—and less interesting—eatery. Far more tragic is the tale of RBJ's Restaurant in Crookston; this establishment abandoned its Bigfoot decor (including an eight-foot hairy replica at the entrance!) for a country theme. Wow, that's original.

And what about the concrete menagerie John Poppin built to decorate his home near Reading? Ask all you want—nobody in town remembers him or his cement critters. At least locals remember what happened to the gigantic, car-washing octopus on University Avenue in Minneapolis: "Oh, they tore that down a while ago," said a disinterested neighbor. If all the locals shared that don't-give-a-damn attitude, it's no wonder the thing disappeared!

Other tourist attractions have been sacrificed on the altar of changing public tastes. Take the Infant House at the Wonderland Amusement Park. No longer are cotton candy–encrusted patrons able to gawk at preemie babies through the windows of a walk-through maternity ward. And what ever happened to Thrill Day, the most popular event at the Minnesota State Fair during the 1920s? Spectators watched as daredevils walked on the wings of biplanes, motorcyclists drove through flaming tunnels, cars smashed into brick walls, airplanes flew into the sides of barns, and high-divers set themselves on fire before taking their death-defying plunges. For the grand finale, two fully loaded trains would crash head-on into each other in front of the stands. Now *that* was entertainment!

It's all too sad to contemplate. If the message isn't clear by now, here it is in black and white: Go. See Minnesota's weird and wonderful attractions while you still can. How long will Menahga's St. Urho statue stand along Route 71, pitchfork and impaled grasshopper in hand? The truth is, nobody knows. See him now—you can't afford to miss it!

ACKNOWLEDGMENTS

*I*n 1917, my great-great-grandparents, Joseph and Margaret Pohlen, were living in Hospers, Iowa, when the United States entered what would later be called World War I. Joseph had emigrated from Germany in 1867, becoming a U.S. citizen in 1871, and the thought of having any of his four sons fighting against their relatives distressed him. Devoutly Catholic, he made a pledge to build a chapel in thanksgiving if none of his sons had to go to war.

In the fall of 1918, his son John was drafted, but before he could report for induction, the Armistice was signed. True to his word, Joseph built a chapel in Wanda, Minnesota, completing the work in 1922. The chapel still stands in Wanda today.

The Pohlen chapel.

I had heard this story several times growing up but never had the chance to see the chapel until I worked on this book. The brick structure was about what I expected, simple and sturdy, in a farming town like so many others I'd driven through. And though I may poke fun at the state's eccentric monuments and occasional bizarre history, I can't deny how exceedingly decent Minnesota really is, filled with hundreds of little communities like Wanda, and populated by some of the nicest folks on the planet.

This book would not have been possible without the assistance, patience, and good humor of many individuals. My thanks go out to the following people for allowing me to interview them about their roadside attractions: Bobbette Axelrod (Sister Fun), Anneliese Detwiler (Northfield Historical Society), Deborah J. Frethem and Cynthia A. Schreiner (Twin Cities Tacky Tour), Col. David Hanson (Ft. Riley Military Museum), Angie Harding (Fantasuite Motel), John Hock (Franconia Sculpture Park), Lesley Kadish (Museum of Questionable Medical Devices), Nels Kramer (Paul's Cabin), Frances Lamb (Akeley Paul Bunyan Historical Society), Donald Manea (Molehill/Towers and Gardens of Antiquities), Patti McFarland (Paul Bunyan Amusement Park), Stanley "Slim" Maroushek (Slim's Woodshed), Ken Nyberg (Vining Sculpture Park), Rick Schmidthuber/Steinarr Elmerson (Nordic Inn Medieval B&B), Gerry Stifter (McLeod County Historical Society), Wayne Windschitl (Pavek Museum of Broadcasting), and the friendly volunteers at the Bemidji Tourism Center.

For research assistance, I am indebted to the librarians in the Minnesota communities of Austin, Cloquet, Crookston, Crosby, Duluth, Grand Rapids, Harmony, Hibbing, International Falls (*big* thanks!), Mankato, Minneapolis, Moorhead, Northfield, Owatonna, Pelican Rapids, St. Cloud, St. Paul, and Stillwater. Thanks also to the visitors bureaus and/or chambers of commerce in Akeley, Alexandria, Austin, Bemidji, Bloomington, Chisholm, Dawson, Duluth, Ely, Fergus Falls, Hinckley, Lake City, Luverne, Minneapolis, New Ulm, Northfield, Olivia, Pipestone, Rochester, St. Paul, Sauk Centre, Silver Bay, Two Harbors, Virginia, and Walnut Grove. I was also assisted early on by Darlene Pfister at the *Minneapolis Star-Tribune*; Tiny Tim thanks her from that Tulip Garden in the Sky.

Friends, family members, and complete strangers volunteered (sometimes after excessive badgering on my part) to act as models for the photographs in this book: Jim Frost, Gianofer Fields, Bobbette Axelrod, Alexandra Homstad, Lesley Kadish, Deborah J. Frethem, and Cynthia A. Schreiner. You were all great sports. Thanks as well to Tamsie Ringler for allowing me to use a photo of her mating car art, *Landing on Eros*, from the Franconia Sculpture Park.

To Uncle Mike and Aunt Laurie and all my cousins, cousins-in-law, and all their kids, thanks for introducing me to the Land of 10,000 Lakes all those years ago, and during the fantastic reunions you hosted at Blackduck and Quadna. To Juan Gonzalez and Tim Murphy, Minnesota friends from way back, I hope you enjoy the book.

Thank you, everyone, at Chicago Review Press for your dedication to the Oddball travel series, but especially Cynthia Sherry and Lisa Rosenthal. To Gianofer Fields at WBEZ, Chicago Public Radio, you're a trooper—few could have survived that six-day marathon sightseeing sojourn.

And to Jim Frost, who has seen it all (and more) on these nationwide road trips, thank you for being there.

RECOMMENDED SOURCES

If you'd like to learn more about the places and individuals in this book, the following are excellent sources. The best sources are listed first within each section.

General Minnesota Guides

Great Minnesota Weekend Adventures by Beth Gauper (Black Earth, WI: Trails Books, 2001)

Minnesota Free by Jim Morse (Minneapolis, MN: Nodin Press, 1998)

Quick Escapes from Minneapolis/St. Paul by Jane H. O'Reilly (Guilford, CT: Globe Pequot Press, 2000)

A Treasury of Minnesota Tales by Webb Garrison (Nashville, TN: Rutledge Hill Press, 1998)

Minnesota Off the Beaten Path by Mark Weinberger (Guilford, CT: Globe Pequot Press, 1999)

Minnesota Travel Companion by Richard Olsenius (Minneapolis, MN: University of Minnesota Press, 1982)

Great Little Museum of the Midwest by Christine des Garennes (Black Earth, WI: Trails Books, 2002)

Minnesota (Trivia)

Minnesota Trivia by Laurel Winter (Nashville, TN: Rutledge Hill Press, 1990)

The Minnesota Book of Days by Tony Greiner (Minneapolis, MN: Minnesota Historical Society Press, 2001)

Minnesota Place Names by Michael Fedo (Minneapolis, MN: Minnesota Historical Society Press, 2002)

Minnesota Almanac 2000 by Chris McDermid (ed.) (Taylors Falls, MN: John L. Brekke and Sons, 2000)

Minnesota (Bigfoot, UFOs, etc.)

The M-Files by Jay Rath (Madison, WI: Wisconsin Trails, 1998)

Gigantic Minnesota Statuary

The Colossus of Roads by Karal Ann Marling (Minneapolis: University of Minnesota Press, 1984)

Monumental Minnesota by Moira F. Harris (Minneapolis: Pogo Press, 1992)
Minnesota Marvels by Eric Dregni (Minneapolis: University of Minnesota Press, 2001)

1. Northwest Minnesota
Paul Bunyan
America in Legend by Richard M. Dorson (New York: Pantheon Books, 1973)
American Tall Tales by Mary Pope Osborne (New York: Alfred A. Knopf, 1991)

The Kensington Runestone
The Kensington Runestone is Real by Robert A. Hall, Jr. (Alexandria, MN: Hornbeam Press, 1982)
The Kensington Runestone: New Light on an Old Riddle by Theodore C. Blegen (St. Paul, MN: Minnesota Historical Society Press, 1968)
Crusade to Vineland by Margaret Barry Leuthner (Alexandria, MN: Explorer Press, 1962)

Speaking with the Locals
How to Talk Minnesotan: A Visitor's Guide by Howard Mohr (New York: Penguin, 1987)

St. Urho
The Legend of St. Urho by Joanne Asala (Iowa City, IA: Penfield Press, 2001)

Lake Wobegon
Lake Wobegon Days by Garrison Keillor (New York: Viking, 1985)
The Man from Lake Wobegon by Michael Fedo (New York: Martin's Press, 1987)

Sinclair Lewis
Sinclair Lewis: Rebel from Main Street by Richard Lingeman (New York: Random House, 2002)

2. Northeast Minnesota
Cécile Cowdery's Art
World War II Envelope Art of Cécile Cowdery by Robin Berg (Lakeville, MN: USM, Inc., 1992)

Grasshopper Chapel
The Story of Mary and the Grasshoppers by Robert J. Voigt (Cold Spring, MN: Assumption Chapel, 1991)

Glensheen Mansion Murders
Glensheen's Daughter by Sharon Darby Hendry (Bloomington, MN: Cable Publishing, 1999)
Secrets of the Congdon Mansion by Joe Kimball (Minneapolis, MN: Jaykay Publishing, 1985)

The Duluth Lynchings
The Lynchings in Duluth by Michael Fedo (St. Paul: Minnesota Historical Society Press, 2000)

Dorothy Molter, the Root Beer Lady
Root Beer Lady by Bob Cary (Duluth, MN: Pfeifer-Hamilton, 1993)

Judy Garland
Get Happy by Gerald Clark (New York: Delta, 2001)

Bob Dylan
Dylan in Minnesota by Dave Engel (Rudolph, WI: River City Memoirs, 1997)

The Hinckley Fire
From the Ashes by Grace Stageberg Swenson (St. Cloud, MN: North Star Press, 1979)

Charles Lindbergh
Lindbergh by A. Scott Berg (New York: Putnam, 1998)

Tammy Faye LaValley Bakker Messner
Tammy: Telling It My Way by Tammy Faye Messner (New York: Villard, 1996)
I Gotta Be Me by Tammy Faye Bakker (Harrison, AR: New Leaf Press, 1978)

3. Southwest Minnesota
Saving Private Ryan
Look Out Below! by Francis L. Sampson (One Hundred First Airborne, 1989)

Laura Ingalls Wilder and Walnut Grove
Laura by Donald Zochert (New York: Avon Books, 1976)
On the Banks of Plum Creek by Laura Ingalls Wilder (New York: Harper Trophy, 1937)
The Little House Guidebook by William Anderson (New York: Harper Trophy, 1996)

4. Southeast Minnesota

Spam
Spam: A Biography by Carolyn Wyman (New York: Harcourt Brace, 1999)
Spam-ku by John Nagamichi Cho (New York: HarperPerenial, 1998)
Spam: The Cookbook by Marguerite Patten (London: Hamlyn, 2001)

Wood Carving Museum
Carving the Circus by the Caricature Carvers of America (East Petersburg, PA: Fox Books, 1997)

Jesse James, Cole Younger, and the Northfield Raid
The Northfield Bank Raid by the Northfield Historical Society (Northfield, MN: *Northfield News* Publishing Company, 1995)
Robber and Hero by George Huntington (Northfield, MN: Northfield Historical Society, 1986)
Cole Younger, Last of the Great Outlaws by Homer Croy (Lincoln, NE: University of Nebraska Press, 1956)
The Jesse James Northfield Raid by John Koblas (St. Cloud, MN: North Star Press, 1999)
Jesse James Ate Here by John Koblas (St. Cloud, MN: North Star Press, 2001)
Murder in Minnesota by Walter N. Trenerry (St. Paul, MN: Minnesota Historical Society, 1985)

The Great Sioux Uprising
Over the Earth I Come by Duane Schultz (New York: St. Martin's Press, 1992)
The Great Sioux Uprising by C. M. Oehler (New York: Da Capo Press, 1997)

Cabela's
Cabela's by David Cabela (New York: Paul S. Eriksson, 2001)

The Minnesota Iceman
"The Mysterious Creature in Ice" by Chris Fellner (Holland, PA: *Freaks!*, Issue 8, February 1997)

5. Minneapolis Area

Andrew Cunanan
Vulgar Favors by Maureen Orth (New York: Delacorte Press, 1999)
Death at Every Stop by Wensley Clarkson (New York: St. Martin's Paperbacks, 1997)

Andrew Cunanan: An American Tragedy by the Cunanan Family (Minneapolis, MN: Piper Publishing, 1998)

The Mary Tyler Moore Show
Love Is All Around by Robert S. Alley and Irby B. Brown (New York: Delta, 1989)

The Artist Currently Known as the Artist Formerly Known as Prince
Dancemusicsexromance by Per Nilsen (London: Firefly Publishing, 1999)

Tiny Tim
Songs in the Key of Z by Irwin Chusid (Chicago: A Cappella, 2000)

John Dillinger
John Dillinger Slept Here by Paul Maccabee (St. Paul, MN: Minnesota Historical Society Press, 1995)

Kathleen Soliah/Sara Jane Olson
Soliah: The Sara Jane Olson Story by Sharon Darby Hendry (Bloomington, MN: Cable Publishing, 2002)

Charles Schulz and Peanuts
Good Grief: The Story of Charles M. Schulz by Rheta Grimsley Johnson (Kansas City, MO: Andrews and McMeel, 1989)

Questionable Medical Devices
Quack! by Bob McCoy (Santa Monica, CA: Santa Monica Press, 2000)

The Younger Boys in Prison
History of the Warden's House Museum by the Washington County Historical Society (Stillwater, MN: Self-Published, 2001)
Convict Life at the Minnesota State Prison by Cole Younger (Stillwater, MN: Valley History Press, 1996)
The Story of Cole Younger, by Himself by Cole Younger (St. Paul, MN: Minnesota Historical Society Press, 2000)

INDEX BY CITY NAME

Bena
Big Fish Supper Club, 213

Blackduck
Big Black Ducks, 32

Bloomington
Louis Farrakhan on the One-Woman Hit List, 193
Mall of America, 193

Blue Earth
Jolly Green Giant Statue, 134

Bongards
Big Cow, 100

Brainerd
World's Largest Talking Paul Bunyan, 46

Burnsville
Fantasuite Motel, 195

Calumet
Hill Annex Mine, 72

Camp Ripley Junction
Hitler's Hanky and Cécile's Letters, 48

Center City
Drying Out the Stars, 49

Chisholm
Iron Man Statue and Iron World, USA, 50

Cloquet
Cloquet Voyageur, 81
Frank's Fill-er-Up, 52

Cold Spring
Grasshopper Chapel, 54

Cosmos
Spacey Town, 101

Crane Lake
Crane Lake Voyageur, 81

North Redwood
Lemonade from Lemons, 114

North St. Paul
World's Largest Snowman, 198

Olivia
Big Ear of Corn, 115

Orr
Big Bluefish, 211

Ortonville
Paul Bunyan's Anchor, 116

Ottertail
World's Largest Dragonfly, 28

Owatonna
Cabela's Outfitters, 151
Casey Jones's Locomotive and the P-38s, 150
Jewel Box, The, 151

Pelican Rapids
Minnesota Minnie, 29
World's Largest Pelican, 30

Pelland Junction
Willie the Worm Man, 204

Pequot Lakes
World's Largest Bobber, 204

Pine City
Pine City Voyageur, 82

Pipestone
Pipestone National Monument and the World's Largest Peace Pipe, 117

Preston
Big Brown Trout, 212
Jail House Inn, 153
Mystery Cave (Forestville State Park), 138

INDEX BY SITE NAME